This book belongs to:

LEISURE ARTS, INC.
Little Rock, Arkansas

EDITORIAL STAFF

Vice President and Editor-in-Chief: Anne Van Wagner Childs. *Executive Director:* Sandra Graham Case. *Executive Editor:* Susan Frantz Wiles. *Publications Director:* Carla Bentley. *Creative Art Director:* Gloria Bearden. *Production Art Director:* Melinda Stout. PRODUCTION — *Managing Editor:* Susan White Sullivan. *Senior Editor:* Carla A. Jones. *Project Coordinators:* Stephanie Gail Sharp and Andrea Ahlen. DESIGN — *Design Director:* Patricia Wallenfang Sowers. EDITORIAL — *Associate Editor:* Linda L. Trimble. *Senior Editorial Writer:* Terri Leming Davidson. *Editorial Associates:* Tammi Williamson Bradley, Robyn Sheffield-Edwards, and Darla Burdette Kelsay. *Copy Editor:* Laura Lee Weland. ART — *Book/Magazine Art Director:* Diane M. Hugo. *Senior Production Artist:* Stephen L. Mooningham. *Production Artists:* Mark A. Hawkins, Faith R. Lloyd, and Dana M. Morris. *Photography Stylists:* Christina Tiano Myers, Karen Hall, Sondra Daniel, and Aurora Huston. ADVERTISING AND DIRECT MAIL — *Senior Editor:* Tena Kelley Vaughn. *Copywriters:* Steven M. Cooper, Marla Shivers, and Marjorie Ann Lacy. *Assistant Copywriter:* Dixie L. Morris. *Designer:* Rhonda H. Hestir. *Art Director:* Jeff Curtis. *Artists:* Linda Lovette Smart and Leslie Loring Krebs. *Publishing Systems Administrator:* Cindy Lumpkin. *Publishing Systems Assistant:* Jennifer Isaacs Smith.

BUSINESS STAFF

Publisher: Bruce Akin. *Vice President, Finance:* Tom Siebenmorgen. *Vice President, Retail Sales:* Thomas L. Carlisle. *Retail Sales Director:* Richard Tignor. *Vice President, Retail Marketing:* Pam Stebbins. *Retail Customer Services Director:* Margaret Sweetin. *General Merchandise Manager:* Russ Barnett. *Distribution Director:* Ed M. Strackbein. *Executive Director of Marketing and Circulation:* Guy A. Crossley. *Circulation Manager:* Byron L. Taylor. *Print Production Manager:* Laura Lockhart. *Print Production Coordinator:* Nancy Lister Baker.

CREDITS

PHOTOGRAPHY: Ken West, Mark Mathews, Larry Pennington, and Karen Busick Shirey of Peerless Photography, Little Rock, Arkansas; and Jerry R. Davis of Jerry Davis Photography, Little Rock, Arkansas. COLOR SEPARATIONS: Magna IV Color Imaging of Little Rock, Arkansas. PHOTO LOCATIONS: The homes of Dr. Dan and Sandra Cook, Shirley Held, and Becky Thompson.

Library of Congress Catalog Number 95-81459
Hardcover ISBN: 0-942237-78-1
Softcover ISBN: 1-57486-033-X

INTRODUCTION

With humble reverence, man has long sought the peace and comfort brought by God's holy angels. Biblical accounts of their benevolence, offered in the greatest times of need, have enthralled us through the ages. The Victorians were especially captivated with the heavenly beings, adorning their homes with ornate images of cherubim and seraphim. Today, we share a renewed wonderment for these enchanting guardians and the beauty and serenity they possess. In celebration of these cherished messengers, we present Angels Remembered, a splendid collection of ethereal cross-stitched images. Adapted from vintage greeting cards, lithographs, and painted masterpieces, many of our designs have been paired with timeless prose and inspirational verses that illustrate angelic majesty. You'll delight in stitching a host of gifts and adornments that are sure to become heirlooms. We've even included cross-stitched clothing so you'll never be without the company of a heavenly spirit. Created in love, these splendid designs will be a blessing to you and to all those with whom they're shared.

TABLE OF CONTENTS

	PHOTO	CHART

RAPHAEL'S ANGEL

Raphael's Angel in Frame 6 50-51

LETTER-PERFECT ANGELS

"Welcome" in Frame 8-9 52-59
Monogram Pillow....................................10.....................52
Monogram Box ....10.....................56
Monogram Candle Screen ....11.....................55

GUARDIAN ANGEL

Guardian Angel in Frame 13 60-61

THE FOUR SEASONS

Spring Angel in Frame............................15.....................63
Autumn Angel in Frame..........................16.....................65
Summer Angel in Frame ....16.....................64
Winter Angel in Frame ....17.....................62

DIVINE VIRTUES

Divine Virtues in Frame 18-19 66-67

FLOWERS FROM HEAVEN

Floral Afghan..21.....................69
Violet Bookmark ....22.....................69
Daffodil Plant Poke ....22.....................69
Tulip Candle Tie ....22.....................69
Violet Shower Pillow ....23.....................68

BRIDE'S BLESSING

Bride's Blessing in Frame.......................25 70-71

HEAVEN SENT

Heaven Sent in Frame 27 72-73
Heaven Sent Photo Album ....28.....................74
Angelic Romper ....28.....................75
"Angel of God" in Frame........................29.....................74

	PHOTO	CHART

DEVOTED ESCORTS

Her Devoted Escort Afghan 30 76-77
Her Devoted Escort in Frame 32 76-77
His Devoted Escort in Frame..................................33 78-79

GENTLE CREATURES

Angel and Butterflies in Frame 35 90-91
Angel and Butterfly Porcelain Jar ....36....................93
Angel with Dove in Frame ....36....................94
Angel with Lamb in Frame 37 92-93

HERB ANGEL

Herb Angel in Frame..39 80-81

ANGEL ON MY SHOULDER

Violet Shower Sweater ....41 ....68 & 82
"Angels Can Fly" Sweater ....42....................82
Angel Brooch ....43....................82
"Believe" Sweater...43.............52 & 82

ENCHANTING CHERUBS

Enchanting Cherubs in Frame 45 84-85

HOME SWEET HAVEN

Watchful Angels in Frame......................................47 86-87
Angel Bread Cloth ....48....................89
Journey Angel in Frame...48....................88
Watchful Angel Hanging Pillow..............................49....................87
Angelic Trio Towel ....49....................88
Angelic Porcelain Jar ....49....................89

General Instructions 95-96

Chart on pages 50-51

RAPHAEL'S ANGEL

The enchanting cherubs from Raphael's glorious painting "Sistine Madonna" capture the essence of angelic bliss. Their petite wings, wavy hair, and childlike features have enthralled angel lovers for centuries. Featuring one of the thoughtful little spirits, our detail from that masterpiece is a reminder of the peaceful musings of heavenly beings.

LETTER-PERFECT ANGELS

As they frolic amidst a garden of letters, these cherubic messengers welcome visitors with glad tidings and a blessing for the host. The angelic alphabet can also adorn an array of lovely tokens, including a cloud-soft pillow and a keepsake box.

Be not forgetful to e
enterta in

8

...ain strangers: for thereby some have

...ngels unawares. Hebrews 13:2

*Our lives are albums written
through with good or ill, with
false or true; and as the blessed
angels turn the pages of our
years, God grant they read
the good with smiles, and
blot the ill with tears!*

— JOHN GREENLEAF WHITTIER

Chart on page 52

Chart on page 56

Chart on page 55

GUARDIAN ANGEL

For he shall give his angels charge over thee, to keep thee in all thy ways. They shall bear thee up in their hands, lest thou dash thy foot against a stone.

— PSALM 91:11-12

Chart on pages 60-61

13

THE FOUR SEASONS

Sweet cherubim and seraphim
flit through the shades of time,
Imparting immortal emblems
that endure within our minds,
Of running through the rains and blooms
bare-toed in seasons mild;
Of lolling 'neath the glimmering rays
that beam from summer's child;
Of rolling amid the harvest leaves,
peals of glee and innocent mirth;
Of rejoicing with holly's crimson seed
Anticipating earth's rebirth.

— *TERRI LEMING DAVIDSON*

14

Chart on page 63

*What is beautiful
is a joy for all seasons and
a possession for all eternity.*

— OSCAR WILDE

Charts on pages 62, 64, and 65

DIVINE VIRTUES

Strengthened by the three supreme virtues, we can face any of life's trials. A shield of Faith empowers us to hold steadfast in our beliefs. With Hope, we anticipate only the best of what the future holds. And the greatest gift, eternal Love, comforts us with blessed assurance.

Charts on pages 66 and 67

FLOWERS FROM HEAVEN

Out yonder in the moonlight, wherein God's acre lies,
Go angels walking to and fro, singing their lullabies.
Their radiant wings are folded, and their eyes are bended low,
As they sing among the beds whereon the flowers delight to grow.

— EUGENE FIELD

Charts on page 69

Guardians of jonquils, tulips, and violets, these angels of spring will add their ethereal grace to indoor accents, as well. Embellished with gossamer ribbons, the heavenly helpers create a delightful plant poke, candle tie, and bookmark. A sweet angel collects the shower of flowery blessings that is falling on our soft pillow.

Charts on page 69

Chart on page 68

BRIDE'S BLESSING

As the blushing bride kneels before her wedding altar, the Heavenly Father sends a comforter to answer her earnest prayers for a joyful marriage. Reaching down to caress the maiden's wispy veil, the graceful angel reassures her with the precious verses found in I Corinthians 13: "Love is patient, love is kind. It does not envy, it does not boast, it is not proud. It always protects, always trusts, always hopes, always perseveres. Love never fails."

chart on pages 70-71

HEAVEN SENT

If ever you've cuddled a laughing infant, basked with contentment and peace, then, truly, you have encountered an angel. Babies are among God's most precious gifts, and He surrounds them with the security and love of His watchful guardians.

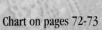

Chart on pages 72-73

They are idols of hearts
and of households;
They are angels of God
in disguise;
The sunlight that sleeps
in their tresses,
His glory still gleams
in their eyes;
These truants from home
and from heaven,
they have made me more
manly and mild;
And I know now how
Jesus could liken
the Kingdom of God to a child.

— CHARLES MONROE DICKINSON

Chart on page 74

Chart on page 75

Chart on page 74

Chart on pages 76-77

DEVOTED ESCORTS

Blissfully unaware of the hidden dangers they may face, children delight in the carefree discovery of nature's adventures. It is comforting to remember that devoted escorts, although unseen, stand ready to gently guide these innocents away from peril with a divine caress.

Angels, where ere we go, Attend our steps whate'er betide.
With watchful care their charge attend, And evil turn aside.

— CHARLES WESLEY

Charts on pages 76-79

GENTLE CREATURES

Keep watch, dear Angel,
and guard with tenderness
small things that have no words.

Chart on pages 90-91

*T*hese adornments honor the
attentive guides who tenderly
protect God's gentle creatures.
Stitched atop a petite jar or
elegantly framed, the designs
remind us of the supreme
love afforded to even the
most delicate beings.

Chart on page 93

Chart on page 94

Chart on pages 92-93

herb angel

Even the tiniest herbs are nourished by the blessings borne from heaven upon the wispy wings of nature's angels. Gently caressing the seeds beneath the soil, the divine gardeners coax forth the tender sprouts that render sweet flavors such as rosemary and basil.

Chart on pages 80-81

ANGEL ON MY SHOULDER

As our guardians flutter unseen about us, they instill uplifting thoughts that provide encouragement throughout the day. These bits of wisdom remind us to approach each day with faith, humor, and high expectations.

Charts on pages 68 and 82

Angels can fly because they take themselves lightly.

Chart on page 82

42

Chart on page 82

Inspire yourself and others with a host of angelic apparel. A feminine accent, this beribboned brooch will be a remembrance of your winged guide. Embellished sweaters offer sweet messages of faith and words of laughter.

Charts on pages 52 and 82

ENCHANTING CHERUBS

Adored for their rosy cheeks and enchanting smiles, playful cherubs such as these delighted the genteel Victorians. Images of the heavenly creatures graced a variety of items, from greeting cards to paintings and tabletop accents. A basket of these angelic innocents will bring a bit of charm to your home.

Chart on pages 84-85

home sweet haven

It's comforting to know that unseen angels are always watching over us, even as we slumber securely in our own homes. While we enjoy the safe haven from a hectic world, our celestial sentries abide in every corner, remaining attentive to our needs and care.

Keep watch
dear Lord
with those who
work or watch
or weep
this night,
and give your angels
charge over
those who sleep.

Chart on pages 86-87

These heavenly designs are sweet reminders that angels linger in every niche of our homes. Offering blessings to all who enter, our array of useful and decorative accents will find their place in the dining room, entry hall, bedroom, or bath.

Chart on page 89

For a good angel
will go with him
This journey will
be successful
and he will
come home
safe and sound
TOBIAS 5:2

Chart on page 88

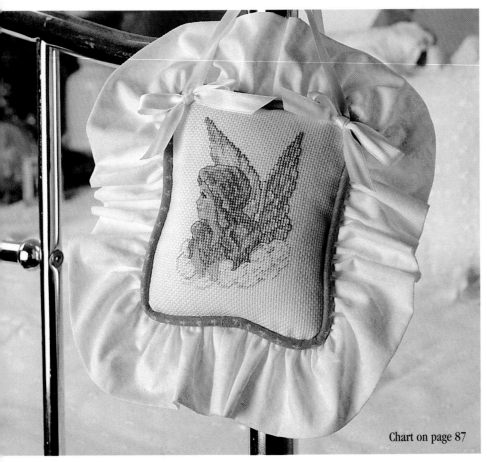

Chart on page 87

Make yourself familiar
with the angels, and behold
them frequently in spirit;
For without being seen,
they are present with you.

— *ST. FRANCIS DE SALES*

Charts on pages 88 and 89

RAPHAEL'S ANGEL

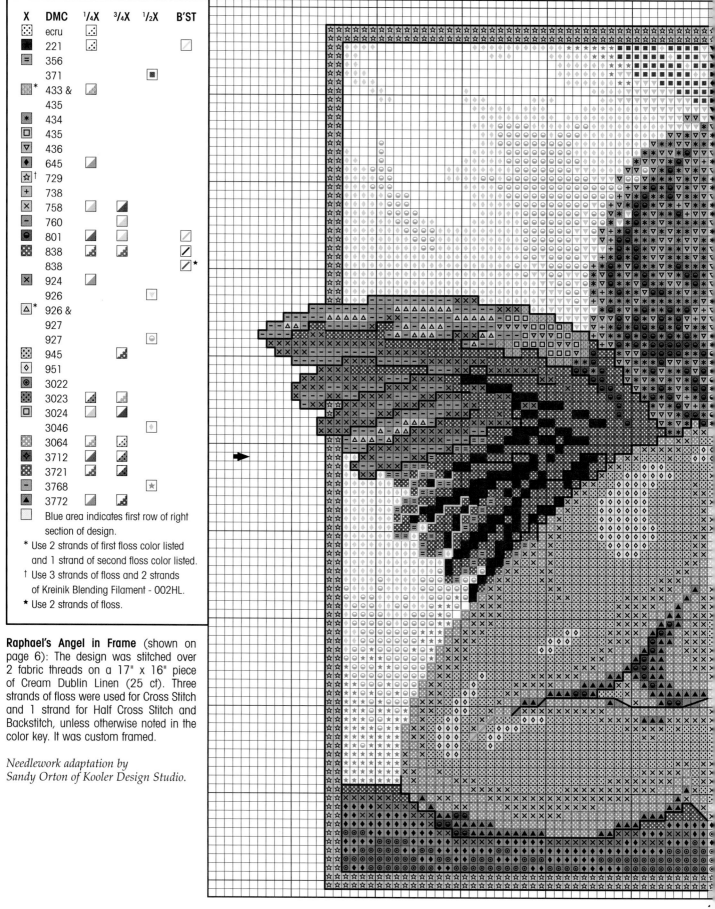

X	DMC	¼X	¾X	½X	B'ST
⊡	ecru	⊡			
■	221				◩
▤	356				
	371			◪	
▨ *	433 &	◩			
	435				
✳	434				
☐	435				
▽	436				
◆	645	◩			
☆ †	729				
+	738				
✕	758	◩	◪		
–	760		◪		
◉	801	◩	◪		◩
▦	838	◪	◪		◪
	838				◪ ★
✕	924	◩			
	926			▽	
△ *	926 &				
	927				
	927			⊙	
⊡	945	◪			
◇	951				
◉	3022				
▨	3023	◩	◪		
☐	3024	◩	◪		
	3046			◆	
▨	3064	◪	◪		
▨	3712	◩	◪		
▨	3721	◪	◪		
▬	3768			★	
▲	3772	◩	◪		

☐ Blue area indicates first row of right section of design.

* Use 2 strands of first floss color listed and 1 strand of second floss color listed.

† Use 3 strands of floss and 2 strands of Kreinik Blending Filament - 002HL.

★ Use 2 strands of floss.

Raphael's Angel in Frame (shown on page 6): The design was stitched over 2 fabric threads on a 17" x 16" piece of Cream Dublin Linen (25 ct). Three strands of floss were used for Cross Stitch and 1 strand for Half Cross Stitch and Backstitch, unless otherwise noted in the color key. It was custom framed.

Needlework adaptation by Sandy Orton of Kooler Design Studio.

STITCH COUNT (107w x 99h)

14 count	7³/₄"	x	7¹/₈"
16 count	6³/₄"	x	6¹/₄"
18 count	6"	x	5¹/₂"
22 count	4⁷/₈"	x	4¹/₂"

Letter-perfect angels

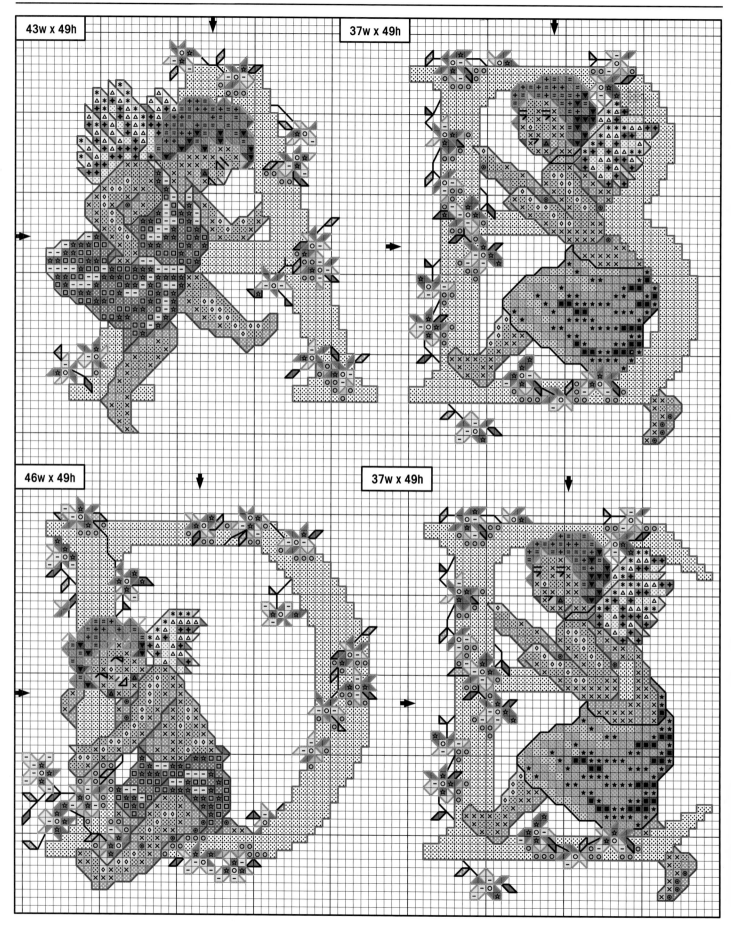

43w x 49h

37w x 49h

46w x 49h

37w x 49h

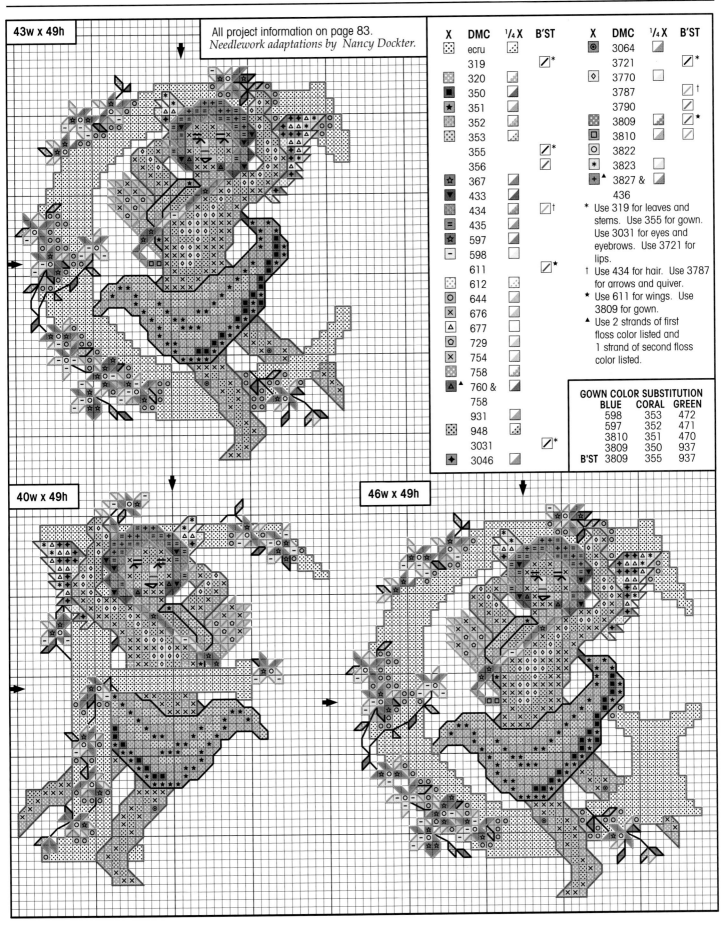

Letter-perfect angels

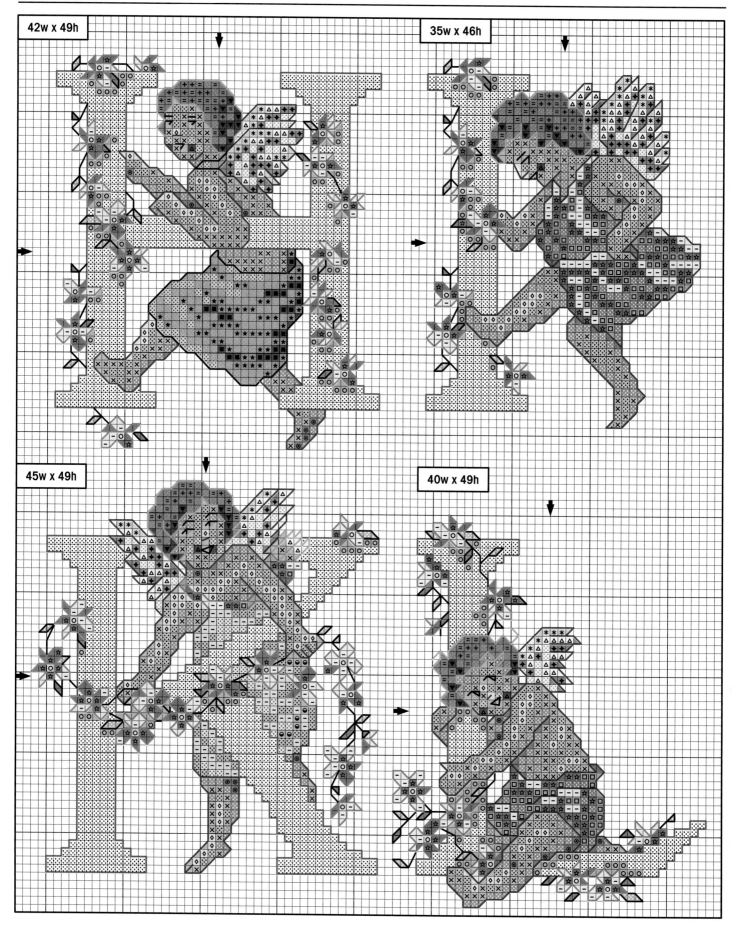

42w x 49h

35w x 46h

45w x 49h

40w x 49h

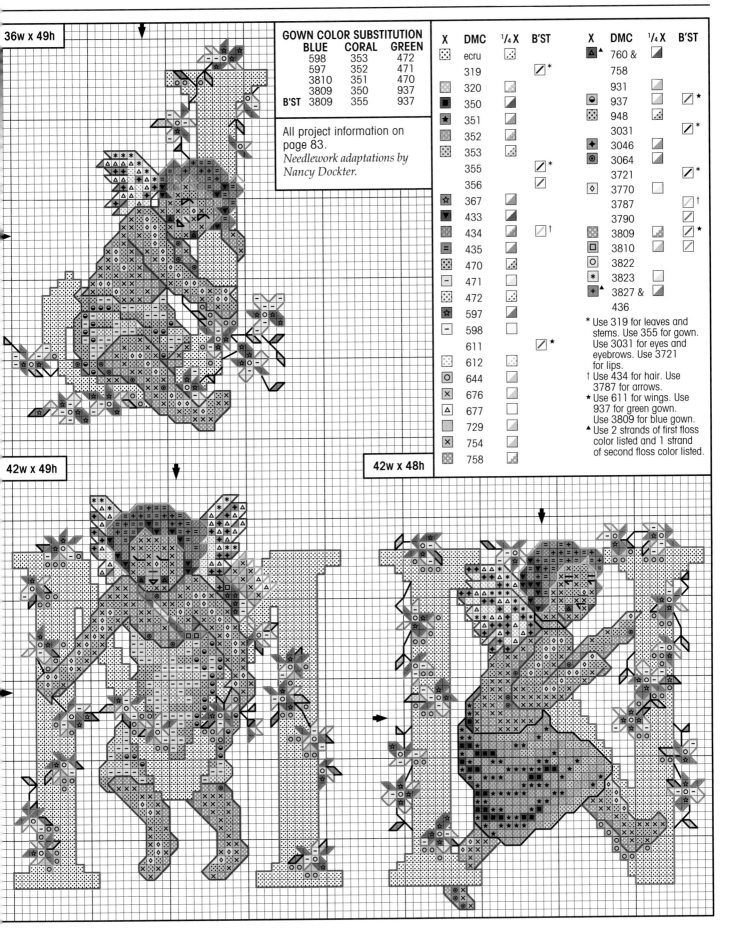

36w x 49h

GOWN COLOR SUBSTITUTION

	BLUE	CORAL	GREEN
	598	353	472
	597	352	471
	3810	351	470
	3809	350	937
B'ST	3809	355	937

All project information on page 83.
Needlework adaptations by Nancy Dockter.

X	DMC	¼ X	B'ST		X	DMC	¼ X	B'ST
	ecru					760 &		
	319		✱			758		
	320					931		
	350					937		★
	351					948		
	352					3031		✱
	353					3046		
	355		✱			3064		
	356					3721		✱
	367					3770		
	433					3787		†
	434		†			3790		
	435					3809		★
	470					3810		
	471					3822		
	472					3823		
	597					3827 &		
	598					436		
	611		✱					
	612							
	644							
	676							
	677							
	729							
	754							
	758							

* Use 319 for leaves and stems. Use 355 for gown. Use 3031 for eyes and eyebrows. Use 3721 for lips.
† Use 434 for hair. Use 3787 for arrows.
★ Use 611 for wings. Use 937 for green gown. Use 3809 for blue gown.
▲ Use 2 strands of first floss color listed and 1 strand of second floss color listed.

42w x 49h

42w x 48h

LETTER-PERFECT ANGELS

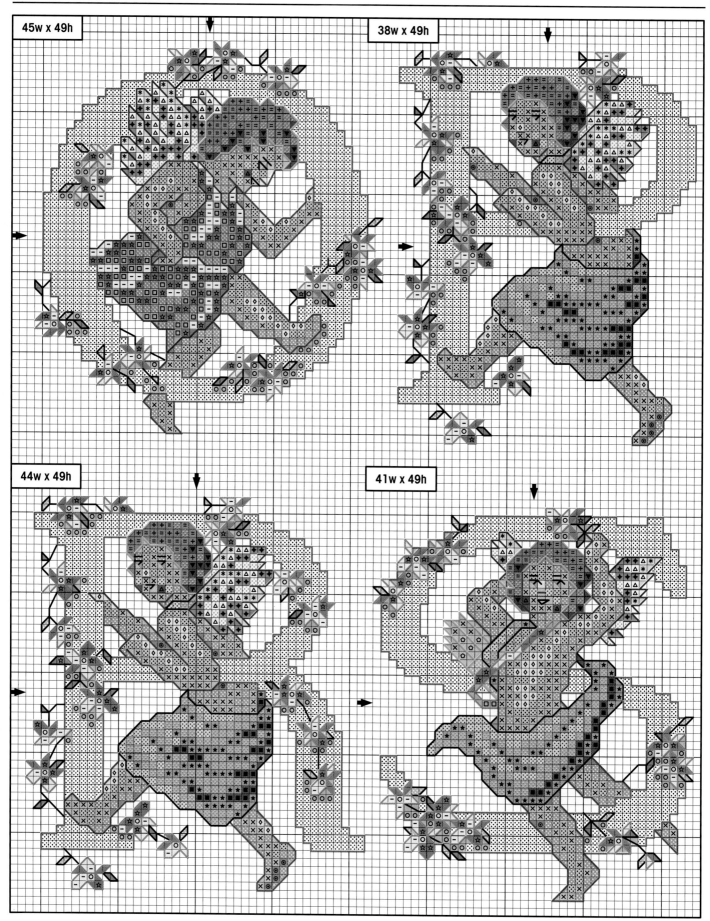

45w x 49h

38w x 49h

44w x 49h

41w x 49h

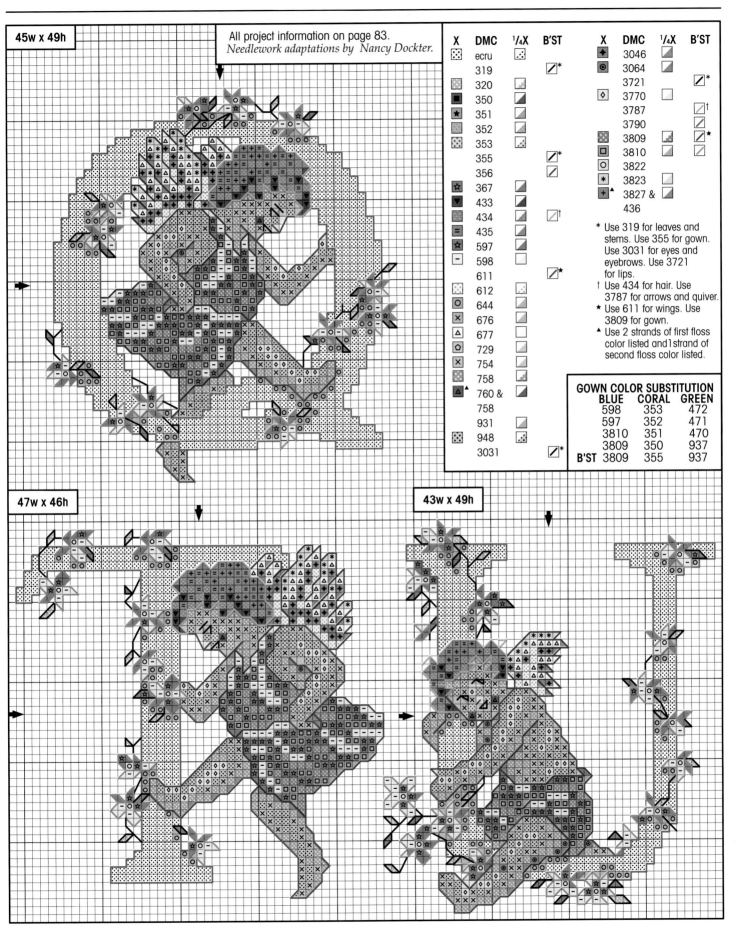

45w x 49h

All project information on page 83.
Needlework adaptations by Nancy Dockter.

X	DMC	¼X	B'ST
▩	ecru	▩	
	319		▧*
▨	320	◩	
■	350	◩	
★	351	◩	
▨	352	◩	
▨	353	◩	
	355		▧*
	356		◩
☆	367	◩	
▼	433	◩	
	434		▧†
≡	435		
☆	597	◩	
−	598		
	611		▧*
▨	612	◩	
○	644	◩	
✕	676	◩	
△	677	◩	
⬠	729	◩	
✕	754	◩	
▨	758	◩	
▲	760 &	◩	
	758		
	931	◩	
▨	948	▩	
	3031		▧*

X	DMC	¼X	B'ST
✚	3046	◩	
◉	3064	◩	
	3721		▧*
◇	3770	▢	
	3787		▧†
	3790		◩
▩	3809	◩	▧*
▢	3810	◩	◩
○	3822	◩	
✳	3823	◩	
✚▲	3827 &	◩	
	436		

* Use 319 for leaves and stems. Use 355 for gown. Use 3031 for eyes and eyebrows. Use 3721 for lips.

† Use 434 for hair. Use 3787 for arrows and quiver.

★ Use 611 for wings. Use 3809 for gown.

▲ Use 2 strands of first floss color listed and 1 strand of second floss color listed.

GOWN COLOR SUBSTITUTION

	BLUE	CORAL	GREEN
	598	353	472
	597	352	471
	3810	351	470
	3809	350	937
B'ST	3809	355	937

47w x 46h

43w x 49h

LETTER-PERFECT ANGELS

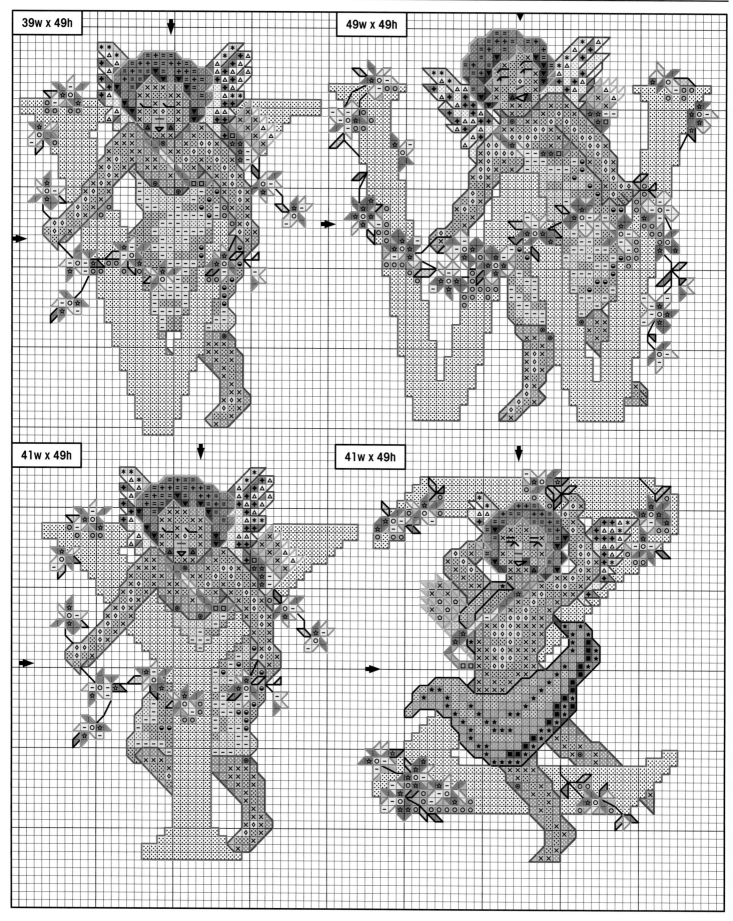

44w x 49h

All project information on page 83.
Needlework adaptations by Nancy Dockter.

GOWN COLOR SUBSTITUTION

	BLUE	CORAL	GREEN
	598	353	472
	597	352	471
	3810	351	470
	3809	350	937
B'ST	3809	355	937

X	DMC	1/4 X	B'ST	X	DMC	1/4 X	B'ST
	ecru				931		
	319		*		937		*
	320				948		
	350				3031		*
	351				3046		
	352				3064		
	353				3721		
	355		*		3770		
	356				3787		†
	367				3790		°
	433				3810		
	434		†		3822		
	435				3823		
	470				3827 & 436		
	471						
	472				3790 French Knot		
	597						
	598						
	611		*				
	612						
	644						
	676						
	677						
	729						
	754						
	758						
	758 & 760						

* Use 319 for leaves and stems. Use 355 for gown. Use 3031 for eyes and eyebrows. Use 3721 for lips.

† Use 434 for hair. Use 3787 for arrows and quiver.

* Use 611 for wings. Use 937 for gown.

▲ Use 2 strands of first floss color listed and 1 strand of second floss color listed.

° Use 2 strands of floss for verse.

Be not forgetful to entertain strangers: for thereby some have entertained angels unawares. Hebrews 13:2

GUARDIAN ANGEL

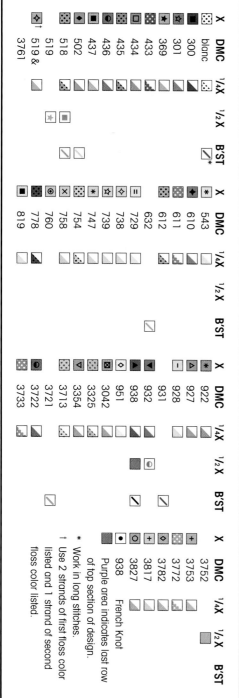

Guardian Angel in Frame (shown on page 13):
The design was stitched over 2 fabric threads on
a 16" x 19" piece of Misty Grey Linen (26 ct).
Three strands of floss were used for Cross Stitch
and 1 strand for Backstitch, Half Cross Stitch,
and French Knots.

*Needlework adaptation by Sandy Orton of
Kooler Design Studio.*

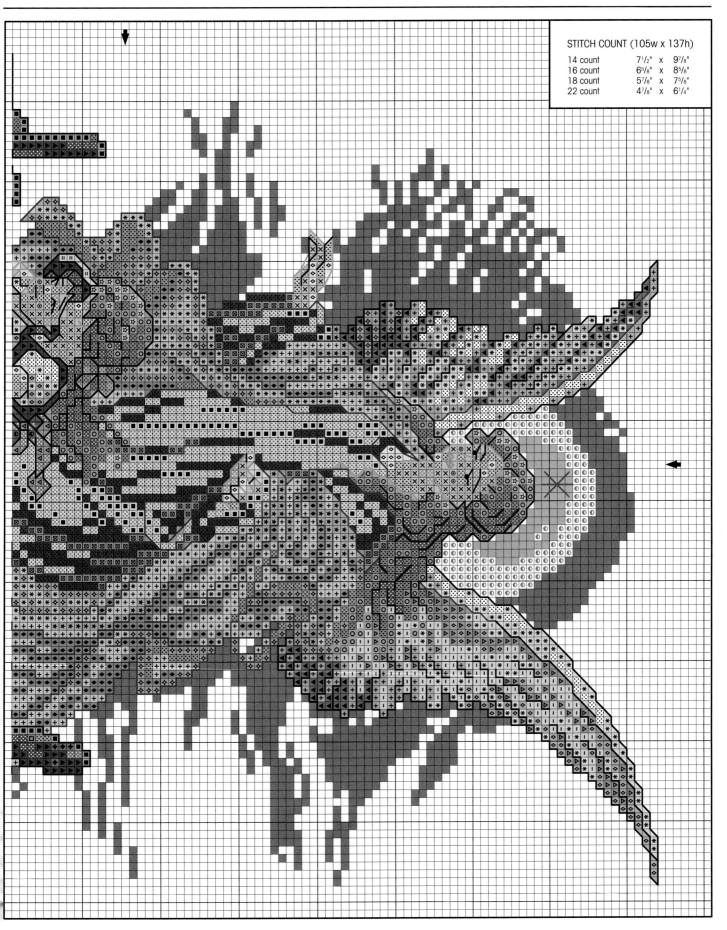

STITCH COUNT (105w x 137h)

14 count	7½"	x	9⅞"
16 count	6⅝"	x	8⅝"
18 count	5⅞"	x	7⅝"
22 count	4⅞"	x	6¼"

the four seasons

X	DMC	¼X	B'ST
▨	blanc	▨	
◖	301	◪	
	310		◪ *
◖	311	◪	◪
✕	319	◪	◪ *
⊙	320		
▨	321	◪	
−	353		
	356		◪ †
◆	367	◪	
□	368		
△	402	◪	
	413		◪ *
✕	451	◪	◪ *
▨	452	◪	
▽	453	◪	
▽	469	◪	◪ *
■	470		
▨	471	◪	
	472		
▲	498	◪	
◈	676		
○	677		
✕	680	◪	◪ ▲
▨	729	◪	
▽	754	◪	
▨	758	◪	
⊕	760		
□	762		
+	772		
−	813		
▨	824	◪	
☆	825	◪	
▨	826	◪	◪ °
◆	838	◪	◪ ▲
▨	839	◪	◪
▨	948	◪	
☆	3064		
	3721		◪ ▲
+	3770		
▨	3776	◪	
◉	3801	◪	
⊙	3827		
	Kreinik Blending		
	Filament - 002	◪ †	
•	310	French Knot	
⊙	Mill Hill Bead - 42013		

* Use 310 for beak. Use 319 for holly. Use 469 for garland leaves.

† Use 356 for flesh. Use Kreinik Blending Filament - 002 for candle flames.

★ Use 413 for dove. Use 451 for angel's wings.

▲ Use 680 for hair. Use 838 for holly branches. Use 3721 for mouth.

° Use 2 strands of floss for candles.

STITCH COUNT (75w x 106h)

14 count	5³⁄₈"	x	7⁵⁄₈"
16 count	4³⁄₄"	x	6⁵⁄₈"
18 count	4¹⁄₄"	x	6"
22 count	3¹⁄₂"	x	4⁷⁄₈"

Winter Angel in Frame (shown on page 17): The design was stitched over 2 fabric threads on a 14" x 16" piece of Cream Cashel Linen (28 ct). Three strands of floss were used for Cross Stitch and 1 strand for Backstitch and French Knots, unless otherwise noted in the color key. Attach beads using 1 strand of DMC 498 floss. See Attaching Beads, page 96. It was custom framed.

Design by Nancy Dockter.

STITCH COUNT (75w x 106h)

14 count	5⅜"	x	7⅝"
16 count	4¾"	x	6⅝"
18 count	4¼"	x	6"
22 count	3½"	x	4⅞"

Design by Nancy Dockter.

X	DMC	¼X	B'ST
⊡	blanc	⊡	
–	ecru		
▲	208		
✦	209		
=	210		
▲	319		
★	327		
+*	353 &		
	760		
	356		◩†
✦	452		
◇	453		
▦*	453 &	⊡	
	452		
▽	471		
	535		◩†
▩	610		◩★
✩	611	◩	
⊠	612	◩	
▽	725	◩	
✴	741		◩★
	744	⊡	
○	746		
✕	754	◩	
▩	758	◪	
○	760	◩	
+	783	◩	
✩	822		
	935		◩
⊡	948	⊡	
■	987	◩	
■	3031	◪	◩
+	3033	◩	
▲	3064	◩	
✕	3078		
○	3347	◩	◩
⊡	3712	◩	
	3721		◩★
⊕	3778	◩	
✚	3781	◩	◩
◦	783		French Knot

* Use 2 strands of first floss
 color listed and 1 strand of
 second floss color listed.
† Use 356 for flesh. Use 535
 for angel's wings.
★ Use 610 for butterfly. Use 741
 for flower centers. Use 3721
 for mouth.

Spring Angel in Frame (shown
on page 15): The design was
stitched over 2 fabric threads
on a 14" x 16" piece of Cream
Cashel Linen (28 ct). Three
strands of floss were used for
Cross Stitch and 1 strand for
Backstitch and French Knots.
It was custom framed.

the four seasons

X	DMC	1/4X	B'ST
⬚	blanc	⬚	
-	353		
	356		╱
★	420	╱	
⊠	434	◩	╱*
▽	435	◩	
⬚	436	◩	
◆	451	╱	╱
◉	452	╱	
	453	╱	
◓	470	╱	
⊠	471	◩	
■	561		╱
⊠	562	◩	╱*
	610		╱
△	644	╱	
+	729		
×	754	╱	
⬚	758	◩	
○	761		
□	762		
▽	772	╱	
☆	813		
-	822		
	824	◢	╱*
◓	826	╱	
◑	869	╱	
✳	913	╱	
	937		╱
⬚	948	◩	
◇ †	954 &		
	955	╱	
◆	976	◢	
⬚	977	◩	
	3031		╱
=	3045		
▲	3064		
◉*	3346		
⬚*	3347		
⊠	3362	╱	╱
+	3363	╱	
◈*	3363		
▬	3364	╱	
□*	3364		
	3721		╱*
◇	3770	╱	
◆	3781	◢	╱*
▽	3821		
○	3822		
×	3827	╱	
○	420	French Knot	

* Use 434 for hair. Use 562 for dress.
Use 824 for flowers. Use 3721 for mouth.
Use 3781 for eyes and eyebrows.

† Use 2 strands of first floss color listed and
1 strand of second floss color listed.

★ Use 1 strand of floss.

STITCH COUNT (72w x 106h)

14 count	5¼" x	7⅝"
16 count	4½" x	6⅝"
18 count	4" x	6"
22 count	3⅜" x	4⅞"

Summer Angel in Frame (shown on page 16): The design was stitched over 2 fabric threads on a 14" x 16" piece of Cream Cashel Linen (28 ct). Three strands of floss were used for Cross Stitch and 1 strand for Backstitch and French Knots, unless otherwise noted in the color key. It was custom framed.

Design by Nancy Dockter.

STITCH COUNT (72w x 112h)		
14 count	5¼"	x 8"
16 count	4½"	x 7"
18 count	4"	x 6¼"
22 count	3⅜"	x 5⅛"

X	DMC	¼X	B'ST
⊠	blanc		
★	ecru	◢	
+	318		
◯	353		
	356		◸
=	370	◢	
	413		◸
▲	414	◢	
▨	420	◢	
▨	433	◢	
▨	434	◢	
▼	435	◢	
★	436	◢	
	632		◸
◆	676		
◯	677	◢	
✳	720	◢	
◉	721	◢	
△	722	◢	
+	729	◢	
✕	754	◢	
-	760		
■	762		
◍	869	◢	
	898		◸
▨	919	◢	
★	930	◢	
✕	931	◢	
⊕	932	◢	
▨	948	◢	
◆	3011		
+	3012	◢	
⬡	3013	◢	
	3031		◸
◆	3033	◢	
▨	3051	◢	
■*	3051	◢	
-*	3052	◢	
■	3064	◢	
	3721		◸
◯	3753		
=	3756		
◇	3770	◢	
▢	3782	◢	
★	3823	◢	
▨	3828	◢	
▨	3829	◢	
●	Mill Hill Bead - 00557		
●	Mill Hill Bead - 40557		

* Use 1 strand of floss.

Autumn Angel in Frame (shown on page 16): The design was stitched over 2 fabric threads on a 14" x 16" piece of Cream Cashel Linen (28 ct). Three strands of floss were used for Cross Stitch and 1 strand for Backstitch, unless otherwise noted in the color key. Attach beads using 1 strand of DMC ecru floss; (see Attaching Beads, page 96.) It was custom framed.

Design by Nancy Dockter.

DIVINE VIRTUES

STITCH COUNT (35w x 76h)

14 count	2½"	x	5½"
16 count	2¼"	x	4¾"
18 count	2"	x	4¼"
22 count	1⅝"	x	3½"

STITCH COUNT (34w x 76h)

14 count	2½"	x	5½"
16 count	2⅛"	x	4¾"
18 count	2"	x	4¼"
22 count	1⅝"	x	3½"

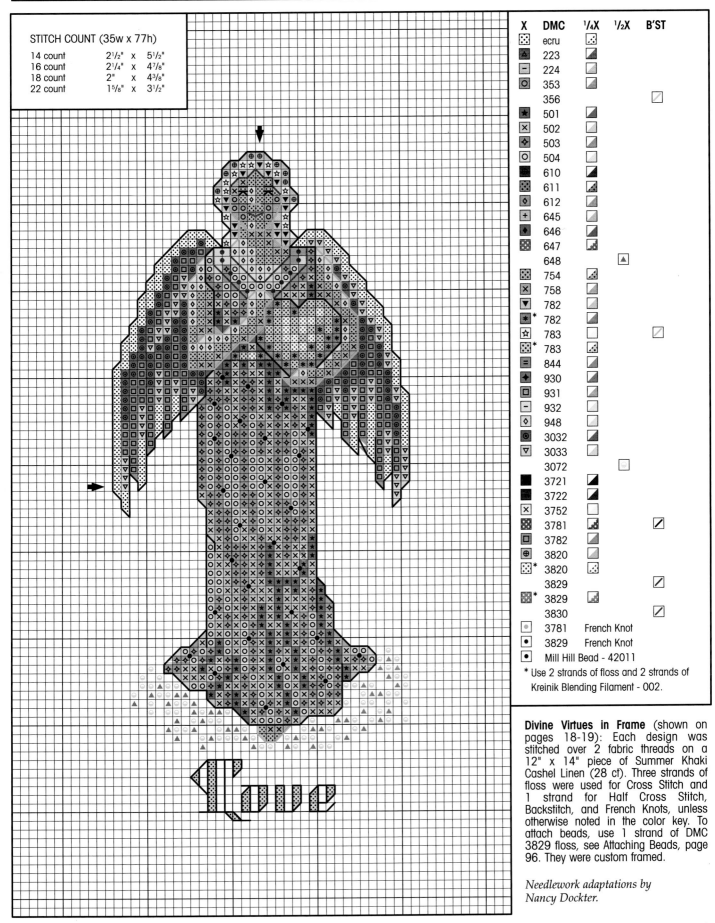

STITCH COUNT (35w x 77h)

14 count	2½"	x 5½"
16 count	2¼"	x 4⅞"
18 count	2"	x 4⅜"
22 count	1⅝"	x 3½"

X	DMC	¼X	½X	B'ST
⊡	ecru	⊡		
▲	223	◤		
–	224	◤		
◉	353	◤		
	356			◹
★	501	◤		
✕	502	◤		
◈	503	◤		
◎	504	◻		
■	610	◤		
▦	611	◢		
◇	612	◤		
+	645	◤		
◆	646	◤		
▨	647	◢		
	648		◸	
⊡	754	◢		
✕	758	◤		
▼	782	◤		
✳*	782	◤		
☆	783	◻		◹
⊡*	783	⊡		
=	844	◤		
✦	930	◤		
◻	931	◤		
–	932	◻		
◇	948	◤		
◉	3032	◤		
▽	3033	◤		
	3072		◻	
■	3721	◤		
■	3722	◤		
✕	3752	◻		
▨	3781	◢		◹
◻	3782	◤		
⊕	3820	◤		
⊡*	3820	⊡		
	3829			◹
▨*	3829	◢		
	3830			◹
◉	3781	French Knot		
●	3829	French Knot		
●	Mill Hill Bead - 42011			

* Use 2 strands of floss and 2 strands of
Kreinik Blending Filament - 002.

Divine Virtues in Frame (shown on pages 18-19): Each design was stitched over 2 fabric threads on a 12" x 14" piece of Summer Khaki Cashel Linen (28 ct). Three strands of floss were used for Cross Stitch and 1 strand for Half Cross Stitch, Backstitch, and French Knots, unless otherwise noted in the color key. To attach beads, use 1 strand of DMC 3829 floss, see Attaching Beads, page 96. They were custom framed.

Needlework adaptations by Nancy Dockter.

flowers from heaven

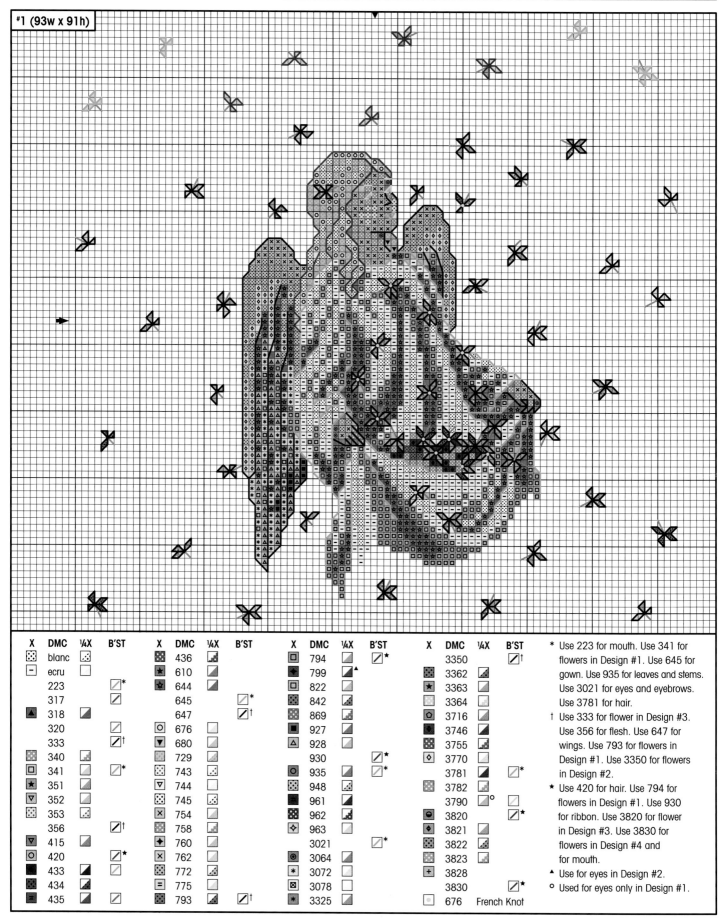

X	DMC	¼X	B'ST		X	DMC	¼X	B'ST		X	DMC	¼X	B'ST		X	DMC	¼X	B'ST
⊠	blanc	⊡			⊠	436	◪			▢	794	◪	▨★			3350		▨†
−	ecru	▢			★	610	◪			✦	799	◪▲			⊠	3362	◪	
	223		▨*		☆	644	◪			▢	822	◪			★	3363	◪	
	317		▨			645		▨*		⊠	842	◪			▢	3364	◪	
▲	318	◪				647		▨†		⊠	869	◪			⬡	3716	◪	
	320		▨		▢	676	▨			▣	927	◪			◼	3746	◪	
	333		▨†		▼	680	▨			△	928	◪			⊠	3755	◪	
⊠	340	◪				729	▨				930		▨★		◇	3770	▢	
▢	341	◪	▨*		▽	744	▢			⊙	935		▨★			3781	◪	▨*
★	351	◪			⊡	743	⊡			⊠	948	⊡			▢	3782	◪	
▽	352	◪			⊡	745	⊡			◼	961	◪				3790	◪⊙	▢
⊠	353	⊡			⊠	754	◪			⊠	962	◪			⊖	3820		▨*
	356		▨†		⊠	758	◪			✦	963	◪			◆	3821		
▽	415	◪			✦	760	◪				3021		▨*		⊠	3822	◪	
⊙	420	◪	▨★		⊠	762	◪			⊙	3064	◪			⊠	3823	◪	
	433	◪	▨		⊠	772	◪			✳	3072	◪			+	3828	◪	
⊠	434	◪			=	775	◪			⊠	3078	▢				3830		▨*
⊠	435	◪	▨		⊠	793	◪	▨†		✳	3325	◪			⊙	676	French Knot	

* Use 223 for mouth. Use 341 for flowers in Design #1. Use 645 for gown. Use 935 for leaves and stems. Use 3021 for eyes and eyebrows. Use 3781 for hair.

† Use 333 for flower in Design #3. Use 356 for flesh. Use 647 for wings. Use 793 for flowers in Design #1. Use 3350 for flowers in Design #2.

★ Use 420 for hair. Use 794 for flowers in Design #1. Use 930 for ribbon. Use 3820 for flower in Design #3. Use 3830 for flowers in Design #4 and for mouth.

▲ Use for eyes in Design #2.

⊙ Used for eyes only in Design #1.

#2 (41w x 41h)

#3 (41w x 41h)

#4 (41w x 41h)

#5 (41w x 41h)

Diagram

	2	
4		3
	5	
3		4
	2	

Violet Shower Pillow (shown on page 23): Design #1 was stitched over 2 fabric threads on a 14" square of Cream Cashel Linen (28 ct). Three strands of floss were used for Cross Stitch and 1 strand for Backstitch and French Knots. To complete pillow, see Violet Shower Pillow Finishing, page 89.

Floral Afghan (shown on page 21): Designs #2-#5 were each stitched over 2 fabric threads on a 45" x 58" piece of White All-Cotton Anne Cloth (18 ct).

For afghan, cut off selvages of fabric; measure 8" from raw edge of fabric and pull out 1 fabric thread. Fringe fabric up to missing fabric thread. Repeat for each side. Tie an overhand knot at each corner with 4 horizontal and 4 vertical fabric threads. Working from corners, use 8 fabric threads for each knot until all threads are knotted.

Refer to Diagram for placement of designs on fabric; use 6 strands of floss for Cross Stitch and 2 strands for Backstitch.

Tulip Candle Tie (shown on page 22): Design #2 was stitched on a 9" square of Antique White Aida (16 ct). Two strands of floss were used for Cross Stitch and 1 strand for Backstitch. To complete candle tie, see Tulip Candle Tie Finishing, page 87.

Daffodil Plant Poke (shown on page 22): Design #5 was stitched on a 9" square of Antique White Aida (16 ct). Two strands of floss were used for Cross Stitch and 1 strand for Backstitch. To complete plant poke, see Daffodil Plant Poke Finishing, page 87.

Violet Bookmark (shown on page 22): Design #3, omitting border, was stitched on a 9" square of Antique White Aida (16 ct). Two strands of floss were used for Cross Stitch and 1 strand for Backstitch. To complete bookmark, see Violet Bookmark Finishing, page 87.

Needlework adaptations by Nancy Dockter.

BRIDE'S BLESSING

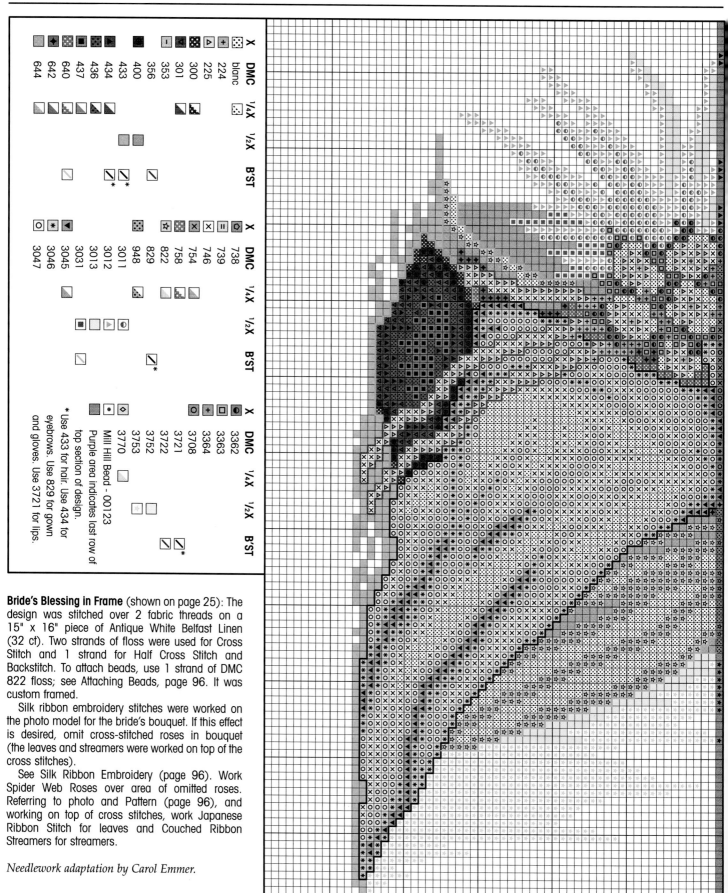

Bride's Blessing in Frame (shown on page 25): The design was stitched over 2 fabric threads on a 15" x 16" piece of Antique White Belfast Linen (32 ct). Two strands were used for Cross Stitch and 1 strand for Half Cross Stitch and Backstitch. To attach beads, use 1 strand of DMC 822 floss; see Attaching Beads, page 96. It was custom framed.

Silk ribbon embroidery stitches were worked on the photo model for the bride's bouquet. If this effect is desired, omit cross-stitched roses in bouquet (the leaves and streamers were worked on top of the cross stitches).

See Silk Ribbon Embroidery (page 96). Work Spider Web Roses over area of omitted roses. Referring to photo and Pattern (page 96), and working on top of cross stitches, work Japanese Ribbon Stitch for leaves and Couched Ribbon Streamers for streamers.

Needlework adaptation by Carol Emmer.

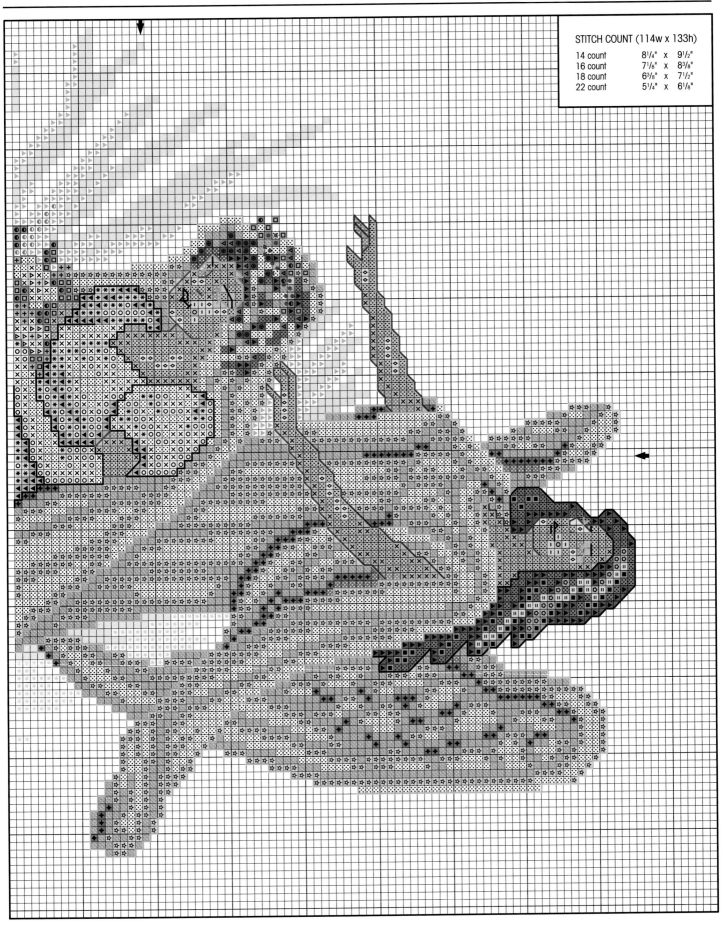

STITCH COUNT (114w x 133h)

14 count	8¼"	x	9½"
16 count	7⅛"	x	8⅜"
18 count	6⅜"	x	7½"
22 count	5¼"	x	6⅛"

HEAVEN SENT

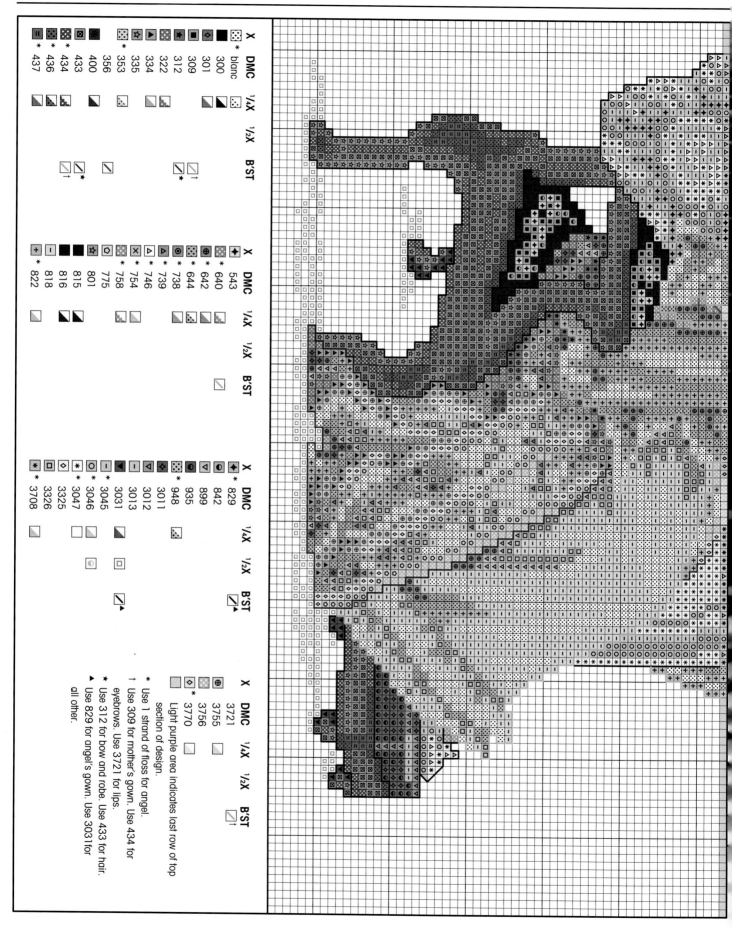

X	DMC	1/4X	1/2X	B'ST
*	blanc			
	300			
	301			
	309			* †
	312			
	322			
	334			
	335	*		
	353			
	356			
	400			
	433			
	434			*
	436			
	437			

X	DMC	1/4X	1/2X	B'ST
+	543			
I	640			
	642	*		
	644	*		
	738			
*	739			
	746			
	754	*		
*	758			
	775			
	801			
	815			
	816			
	818			
*	822			

X	DMC	1/4X	1/2X	B'ST
*	829			
	842			
	899			
	935			
*	948			
	3011			
	3012			
	3013			
	3031			▲
	3045			
	3046			
*	3047			
	3325			
	3326			
*	3708			

X	DMC	1/4X	1/2X	B'ST
*	3721			†
⊕	3755			
	3756			
*	3770			

Light purple area indicates last row of top section of design.

* Use 1 strand of floss for angel.
† Use 309 for mother's gown. Use 434 for eyebrows. Use 3721 for lips.
★ Use 312 for bow and robe. Use 433 for hair.
▲ Use 829 for angel's gown. Use 3031 for all other.

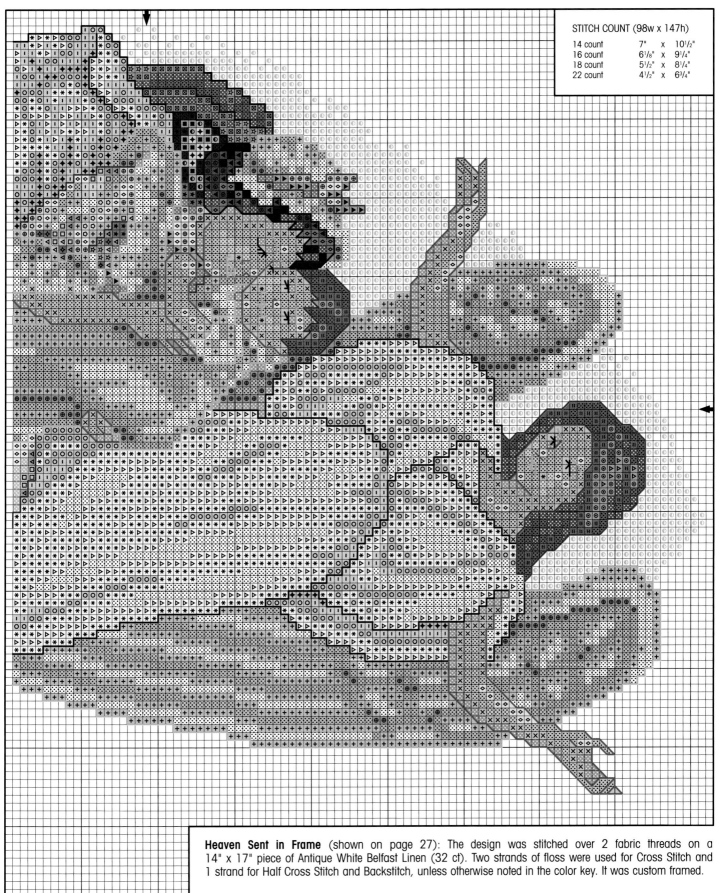

STITCH COUNT (98w x 147h)

14 count	7"	x 10½"
16 count	6⅛"	x 9¼"
18 count	5½"	x 8¼"
22 count	4½"	x 6¾"

Heaven Sent in Frame (shown on page 27): The design was stitched over 2 fabric threads on a 14" x 17" piece of Antique White Belfast Linen (32 ct). Two strands of floss were used for Cross Stitch and 1 strand for Half Cross Stitch and Backstitch, unless otherwise noted in the color key. It was custom framed.

Needlework adaptation by Carol Emmer.

DESIGN #1
STITCH COUNT (97w x 100h)

14 count	7"	x	7¼"
16 count	6⅛"	x	6¼"
18 count	5½"	x	5⅝"
22 count	4½"	x	4⅝"

Angel of God

My guardian dear,

To whom God's love commits me here.

Ever this day be at my side

To light and guard, to rule and guide.

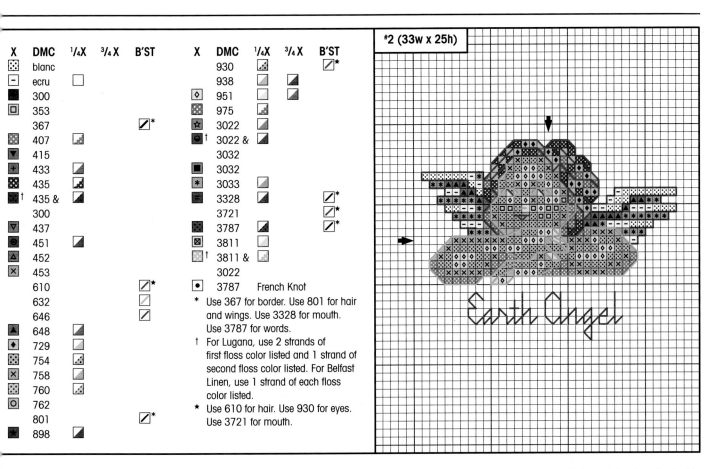

#2 (33w x 25h)

X	DMC	¼X	¾X	B'ST	X	DMC	¼X	¾X	B'ST
⊡	blanc					930	◢		◪*
-	ecru	☐				938		◪	
■	300				◇	951		◪	
▣	353				▨	975	◢		
	367			◪*	★	3022		◪	
▨	407	◢			◉†	3022 & 3032		◪	
▼	415				■	3032			
+	433	◪			✳	3033		◪	
▨	435	◢			▧	3328	◪		◪*
■†	435 & 300	◪				3721			◪*
▼	437				▨	3787	◢		◪*
◉	451	◪			⊠	3811	☐		
▲	452				▨†	3811 & 3022	◢		
✕	453				•	3787		French Knot	
	610			◪*					
	632			◪					
	646			◪					
▲	648	◪							
◆	729	◢							
▨	754	◢							
✕	758	◢							
▨	760	◢							
○	762								
	801			◪*					
▨	898		◪						

* Use 367 for border. Use 801 for hair and wings. Use 3328 for mouth. Use 3787 for words.

† For Lugana, use 2 strands of first floss color listed and 1 strand of second floss color listed. For Belfast Linen, use 1 strand of each floss color listed.

* Use 610 for hair. Use 930 for eyes. Use 3721 for mouth.

"Angel of God" in Frame (shown on page 29): Design #1 was stitched over 2 fabric threads on a 16" square of Antique White Lugana (25 ct). Three strands of floss were used for Cross Stitch and 1 strand for Backstitch and French Knots. It was custom framed.

Heaven Sent Photo Album (shown on page 28): The angel and cloud from Design #1 were stitched over 2 fabric threads on a 21" x 9" piece of Antique White Belfast Linen (32 ct). Two strands of floss were used for Cross Stitch and 1 strand for Backstitch. Center design vertically with right edge of design 4¾" from short edge.

For album, you will need a 7¼" x 4⅝" photo album, 14" x 4½" piece of batting, two 5½" x 5½" pieces of lightweight white fabric for lining, two 6¼" x 4" pieces of poster board, two 7" lengths of 1⅜"w flat trim, two 14" lengths of ¼"w ribbon, two 14" lengths each of two different colors of ⅛"w ribbon, and clear-drying craft glue.

Trim stitched piece to 16¾" x 6¼", centering design vertically with right edge of design 3¼" from short edge.

Glue batting to outside of album. Centering stitched design on front of album, place album batting side down on wrong side of stitched piece. Fold linen at corners to inside of album and glue in place. At center bottom of album, turn a 2" section of linen ⅜" to wrong side (**Fig. 1**); glue folded edge to inside of album. Repeat at center top of album. Fold remaining edges of linen to inside of album and glue in place; allow to dry.

Referring to photo, glue lengths of flat trim to front cover of album. For ties, match short ends of one length of each ribbon and tie together with an overhand knot 2" from one end; trim ribbon ends as desired. Glue unknotted ends of ribbons to inside of front cover. Repeat with remaining ribbon lengths for inside of back cover.

Center one piece of poster board on wrong side of one lining fabric piece; fold fabric at corners to back of poster board and glue in place. Fold edges of fabric to back of poster board and glue in place. Glue wrong side of covered poster board to inside of front cover of album approximately ¼" from top, bottom, and outside edge of album. Repeat with remaining

poster board and lining fabric piece for inside of back cover.

Referring to photo, tie ribbons in a bow.

Fig. 1

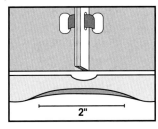

2"

Needlework adaptation by Vicky D'Agostino, Victoria's Needle.

Angelic Romper (shown on page 28): Design #2 was stitched over a 7" x 6" piece of 12 mesh waste canvas on a purchased romper with top of design ⅞" below neckline seam. Three strands of floss were used for Cross Stitch and 1 strand for Backstitch. See Working on Waste Canvas, page 83.

Needlework adaptation by Jane Chandler.

DEVOTED ESCORTS

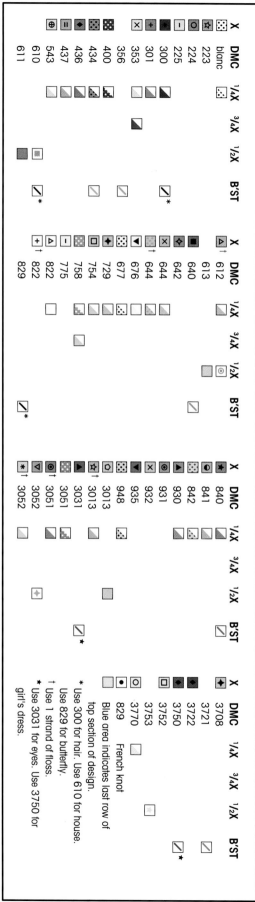

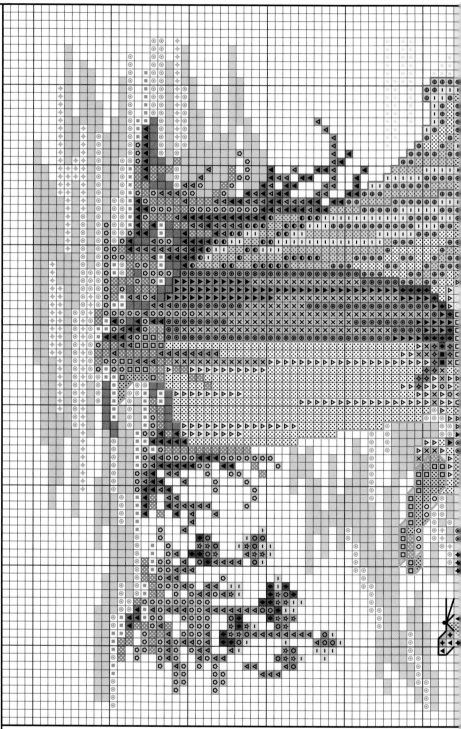

Her Devoted Escort in Frame (shown on page 32): The design was stitched over 2 fabric threads on a 14" x 16" piece of Cream Belfast Linen (32 ct). Two strands of floss were used for Cross Stitch and 1 strand for Half Cross Stitch, Backstitch, and French Knot, unless otherwise noted in the color key. It was custom framed.

Her Devoted Escort Afghan (shown on page 30): A portion of the design (refer to photo and Diagram) was stitched over 2 fabric threads on a 45" x 58" piece of Ivory All-Cotton Anne Cloth (18 ct).

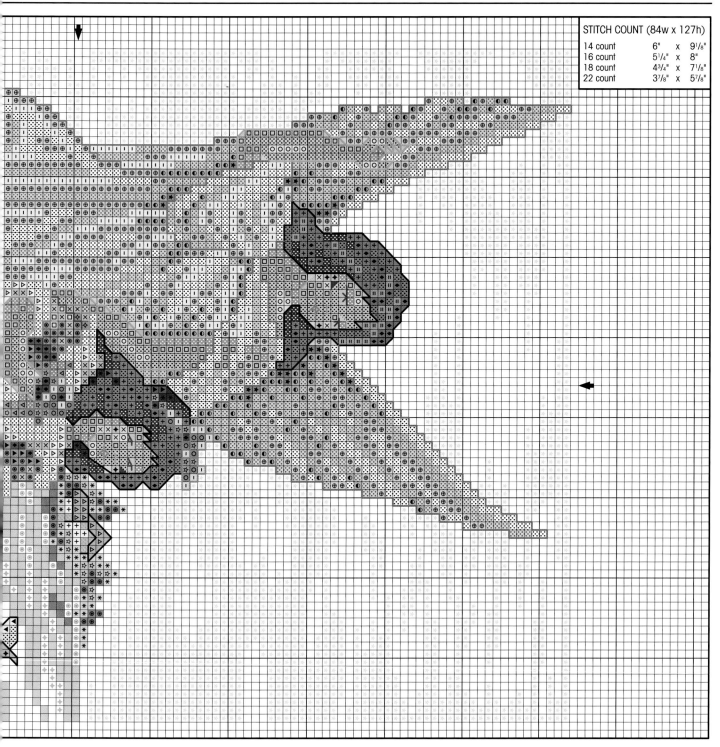

STITCH COUNT (84w x 127h)

14 count	6"	x	9 1/8"
16 count	5 1/4"	x	8"
18 count	4 3/4"	x	7 1/8"
22 count	3 7/8"	x	5 7/8"

For afghan, cut off selvages of fabric; measure 5 1/2" from raw edge of fabric and pull out fabric thread. Fringe fabric up to missing fabric thread. Repeat for each side. Tie an overhand knot at each corner with 4 horizontal and 4 vertical fabric threads. Working from corners, use fabric threads for each knot until all threads are knotted.

Refer to Diagram for placement of design on fabric; use 6 strands of floss for Cross Stitch and strands for Backstitch and French Knot unless otherwise noted in the color key.

eedlework adaptation by Carol Emmer.

Diagram

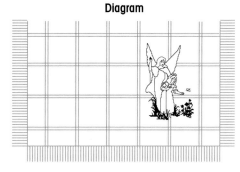

Devoted escorts

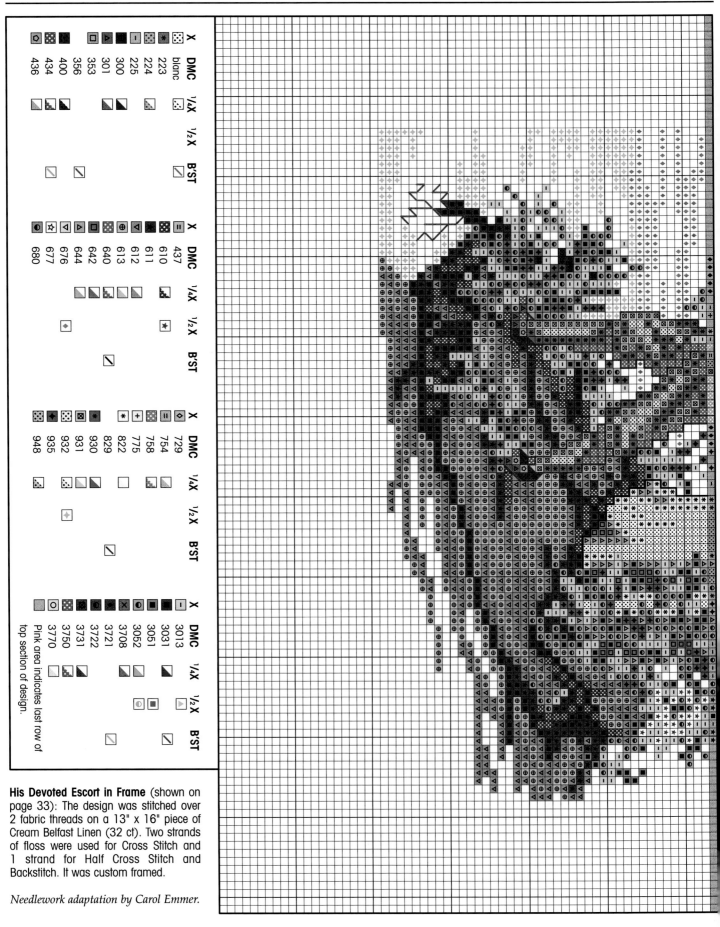

X	DMC	1/4X	1/2X	B'ST
◔	blanc			
▧	223			
▨	224			
▣	225	▨		▨
▶	300			
■	301	▨		▨
▮	353			
▨	356			
✳	400	▨		
▨	436	▨		

X	DMC	1/4X	1/2X	B'ST
◑	437			
✿	610			
◁	611	▨		
▶	612			
▣	613	▨	◆	
▨	640		✦	
⊕	642			
◀	644			
▨	676	▨		�ₙ
▥	677			
‖	680			

X	DMC	1/4X	1/2X	B'ST
▨	729			
◆	754			
▨	758	◆		
▨	775			
‖	822	▥		
◇	829	□		
✳	930	▨		
✛	931	▨		
▨	932		✦	
▨	935	▨		◥
▨	948	◔		

X	DMC	1/4X	1/2X	B'ST
▨	3013			
▧	3031			
▨	3051	▨		
▨	3052	▨		
✕	3708	▨		
◐	3721	▨	◑	
■	3722	▨	■	
■	3731	▨		
▮	3750	▨	▶	◥
◘	3770	▨		

Pink area indicates last row of top section of design.

His Devoted Escort in Frame (shown on page 33): The design was stitched over 2 fabric threads on a 13" x 16" piece of Cream Belfast Linen (32 ct). Two strands of floss were used for Cross Stitch and 1 strand for Half Cross Stitch and Backstitch. It was custom framed.

Needlework adaptation by Carol Emmer.

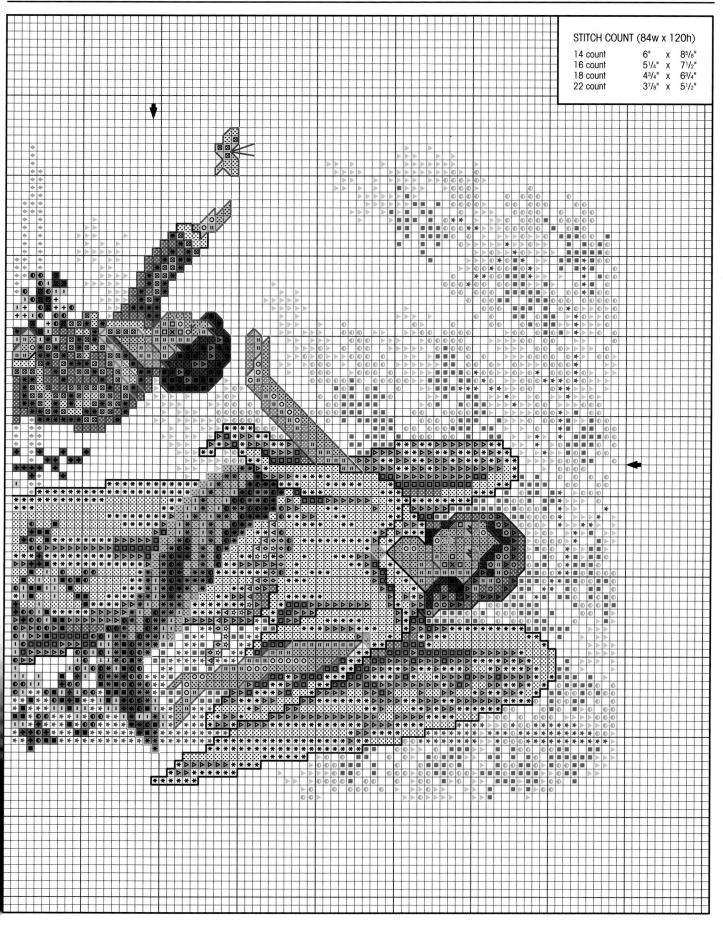

HERB ANGEL

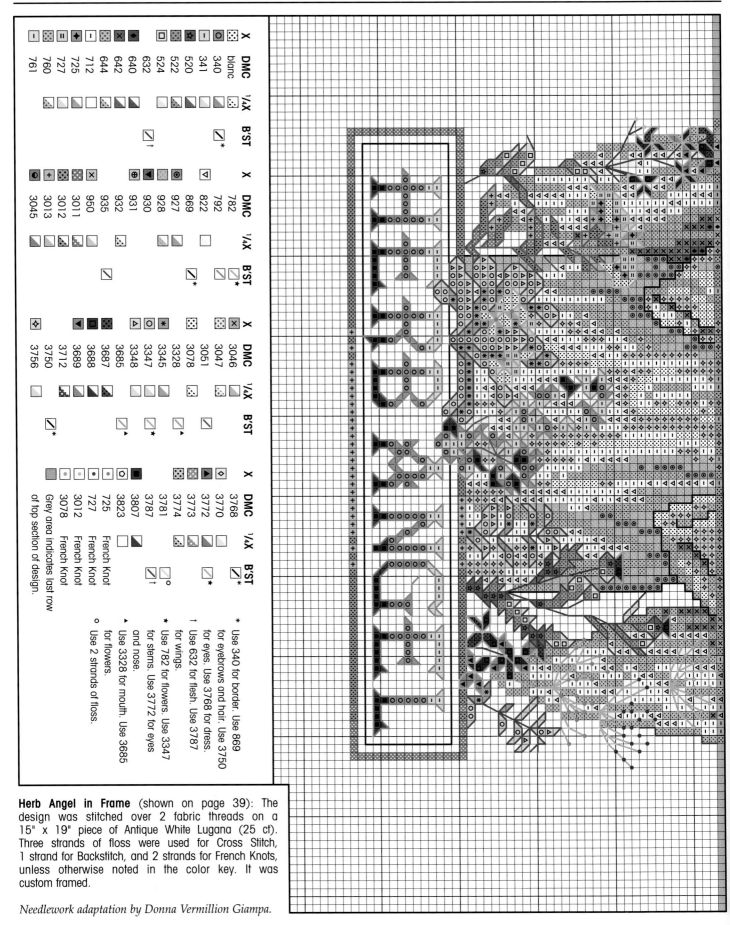

X	DMC	1/4X	B'ST
	blanc		
	340		*
	341		
	520		
	522		
	524		
	632		†
	640		
	642		
	644		
	712		
	725		
	727		
	760		
	761		

X	DMC	1/4X	B'ST
	782		
	792		*
	822		
	869		
	927		
	928		
	930		
	931		
	932		
	935		
	950		
	3011		
	3012		
	3013		
	3045		

X	DMC	1/4X	B'ST
	3046		
	3047		
	3051		
	3078		
	3328		▶
	3345		
	3347		★
	3348		
	3685		▶
	3687		
	3688		
	3689		
	3712		
	3750		
	3756		

X	DMC	1/4X	B'ST
	3768		
	3770		
	3772		*
	3773		
	3774		
	3781		
	3787		† °
	3807		
	3823		
	725 French Knot		
	727 French Knot		
	3012 French Knot		
	3078 French Knot		

* Use 340 for border. Use 869 for eyebrows and hair. Use 3750 for eyes. Use 3768 for dress.

† Use 632 for flesh. Use 3787 for wings.

★ Use 782 for flowers. Use 3347 for stems. Use 3772 for eyes and nose.

▶ Use 3328 for mouth. Use 3685 for flowers.

○ Use 2 strands of floss.

Grey area indicates last row of top section of design.

Herb Angel in Frame (shown on page 39): The design was stitched over 2 fabric threads on a 15" x 19" piece of Antique White Lugana (25 ct). Three strands of floss were used for Cross Stitch, 1 strand for Backstitch, and 2 strands for French Knots, unless otherwise noted in the color key. It was custom framed.

Needlework adaptation by Donna Vermillion Giampa.

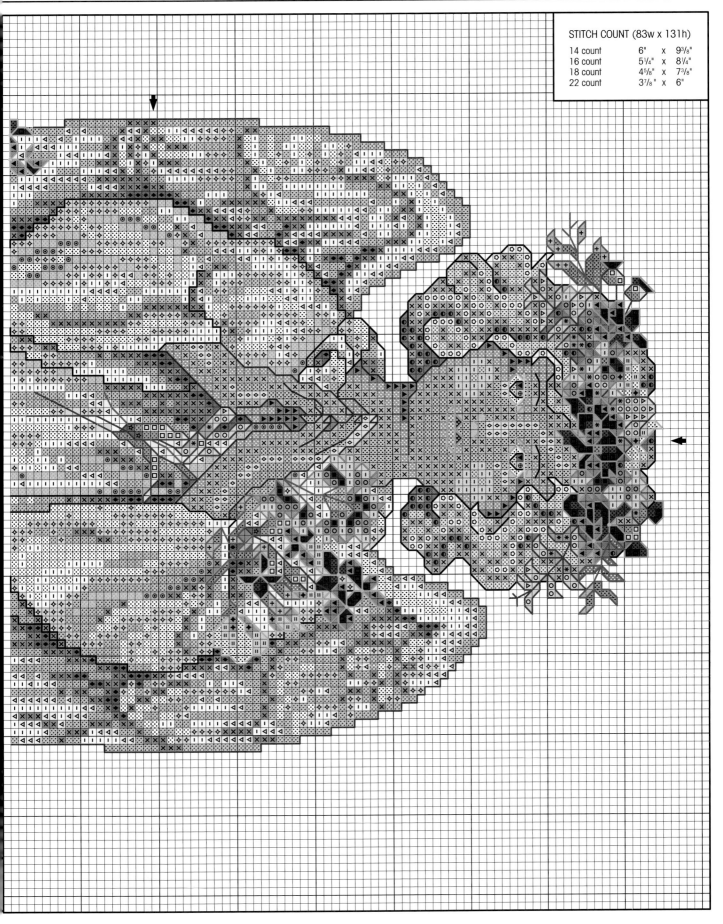

STITCH COUNT (83w x 131h)

14 count	6"	x	9³/₈"
16 count	5¹/₄"	x	8¹/₄"
18 count	4⁵/₈"	x	7³/₈"
22 count	3⁷/₈"	x	6"

ANGEL ON MY SHOULDER

#1 (78w x 47h)

Angels can fly because they take themselves lightly.

X	DMC	¼X	B'ST
○	ecru		
+	320	▨	
	356	▨	▨
▲	367	▨	▨
	433	▨	▨
▨	434	▨	
+	436	▨	
✕	754	▨	
▨	758	▨	
▨	761	▨	
	844		▨
	869		▨
◆	926	▨	
	927	▨	
⌂	928	▨	
◇	948	▨	
⊕	962	▨	
△	963	▨	
◐	3041	▨	
=	3042	▨	
⊠	3045	▨	
○	3046	▨	
◈	3743	▨	
	3746		▨
	3790		▨
●	844	French Knot	
◦	3746	French Knot	

Grey area indicates placement of the letter B from Letter-Perfect Angels, page 52.

#2 (59w x 9h)

Expect a Miracle

#3 (136w x 49h)

olet Shower Sweater (shown on page █; chart on page 68): A portion (refer to █oto) of the Violet Shower design was stitched █th Design #2 over a 9" x 11" piece of █ mesh waste canvas on a purchased █veater with top of Violet Shower design █" below bottom of neckband. Center Design █2 three squares below Violet Shower design. █ur strands of floss were used for Cross Stitch █d 2 strands for Backstitch and French Knots.

█elieve" Sweater (shown on page 43): The █tter B from Letter-Perfect Angels, page █2, was stitched with Design #3 over a █4" x 8" piece of 14 mesh waste canvas on a █rchased sweater with top of design 1" below █ottom of neckband. Three strands of floss █re used for Cross Stitch and 1 strand █r Backstitch.

█eedlework adaptations by Nancy Dockter.

█ngels Can Fly" Sweater (shown on █ge 42): Design #1 was stitched over a █2" x 9" piece of 10 mesh waste canvas on a █rchased sweater with top of design █/4" below bottom of neckband. Five strands █ floss were used for Cross Stitch and █ strands for Backstitch and French Knots.

Angel Brooch (shown on page 43): The left angel only from Design #1 was stitched on a 6" square of Ivory Aida (18 ct). Two strands of floss were used for Cross Stitch and 1 strand for Backstitch.

For brooch, you will need a 6" square of lightweight cream fabric for backing, fabric stiffener, small foam brush, 16" length of ⁵/₈" w wired ribbon, ⁵/₈" heart-shaped charm, and pin back.

To stiffen design, follow Stiffening Instructions below. Referring to photo, cut out stitched design; attach ribbon and charm as desired and trim ribbon ends. Glue pin back to back of design.

Needlework adaptations by Jane Chandler.

STIFFENING INSTRUCTIONS

Apply a heavy coat of fabric stiffener to wrong side of stitched piece using small foam brush. Matching wrong sides, place stitched piece on backing fabric, smoothing stitched piece while pressing fabric pieces together; allow to dry. Apply fabric stiffener to backing fabric; allow to dry.

Working on Waste Canvas: Waste canvas is a special canvas that provides an evenweave grid for placing stitches on fabric. After the design is worked over the canvas, the canvas threads are removed leaving the design on the fabric. The canvas is available in several mesh sizes.

Cover edges of canvas with masking tape. Cut a piece of lightweight non-fusible interfacing the same size as canvas to provide a firm stitching base.

Find desired stitching area and mark center of area with a pin. Match center of canvas to pin. Use the blue threads in canvas to place canvas straight on garment; pin canvas to garment. Pin interfacing to wrong side of garment. Baste all layers together as shown in **Fig. 1**.

Using a sharp needle, work design, stitching from large holes to large holes. Trim canvas to within ³/₄" of design. Dampen canvas until it becomes limp. Pull out canvas threads one at a time using tweezers (**Fig. 2**). Trim interfacing close to design.

Fig. 1   **Fig. 2**

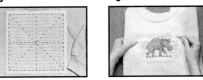

LETTER-PERFECT ANGELS

█te: Each angel's gown is charted in four █ades of either blue, coral, or green. The █wn of any angel may be stitched in any one █ the three colors by following the Gown Color █bstitution list located on the same page as █lor key.

█elcome" in Frame (shown on pages 8-9; █arts on pages 52-59): The word Welcome █s stitched over 2 fabric threads on a █0" x 12" piece of Summer Khaki Cashel Linen █8 ct). Three strands of floss were used for █oss Stitch and 1 strand for Backstitch and █ench Knots, unless otherwise noted in the █lor key. Lower edges of letters were aligned █d letters were spaced according to shape of █sign. Referring to photo, center and stitch the █rse, Hebrews 13:2 (page 59), 3 squares █low WELCOME, with 2 squares between █es of the verse.

█onogram Pillow (shown on page 10; chart █ page 52): The letter A was stitched over █ fabric threads on a 12" square of Antique White Cashel Linen (28 ct). Three strands of floss were used for Cross Stitch and 1 strand for Backstitch. For pillow, you will need a 5¹/₄" x 6" piece of fabric for pillow backing, 4" x 38¹/₂" fabric strip for ruffle, 22" length of ¹/₄" dia. purchased cording with attached seam allowance, and polyester fiberfill.

Centering design, trim stitched piece to measure 5¹/₄" x 6".

If needed, trim seam allowance of cording to ¹/₂"; pin cording to right side of stitched piece, making a ³/₈" clip in seam allowance of cording at corners. Ends of cording should overlap approximately 4". Turn overlapped ends of cording toward outside edge of stitched piece; baste cording to stitched piece.

For ruffle, press short edges of fabric strip ¹/₂" to wrong side. Matching wrong sides and long edges, fold strip in half; press. Machine baste ¹/₂" from raw edges; gather fabric strip to fit stitched piece. Matching raw edges, pin ruffle to right side of stitched piece overlapping short ends ¹/₄". Use a ¹/₂" seam allowance to sew ruffle to stitched piece.

Matching right sides and leaving an opening for turning, use a ¹/₂" seam allowance to sew stitched piece and backing fabric together. Trim seam allowances diagonally at corners; turn pillow right side out carefully pushing corners outward. Stuff pillow with polyester fiberfill and blind stitch opening closed.

Monogram Candle Screen (shown on page 11; chart on page 55): The letter J was stitched over 2 fabric threads on a 10" x 11" piece of Antique White Lugana (25 ct). Three strands of floss were used for Cross Stitch and 1 strand for Backstitch. It was inserted in a 5" x 6¹/₂" candle screen frame (3¹/₂" x 5" opening).

Monogram Box (shown on page 10; chart on page 56): The letter S was stitched over 2 fabric threads on an 11" square of Antique White Lugana (25 ct). Three strands of floss were used for Cross Stitch and 1 strand for Backstitch. It was inserted in the lid of a 6" square wooden box (5" square opening).

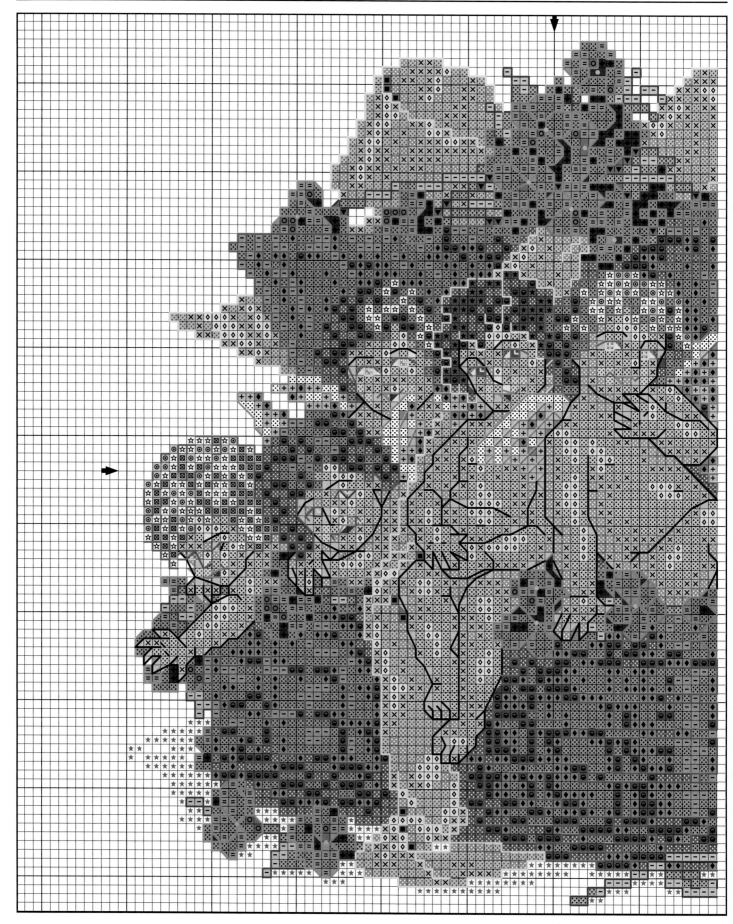

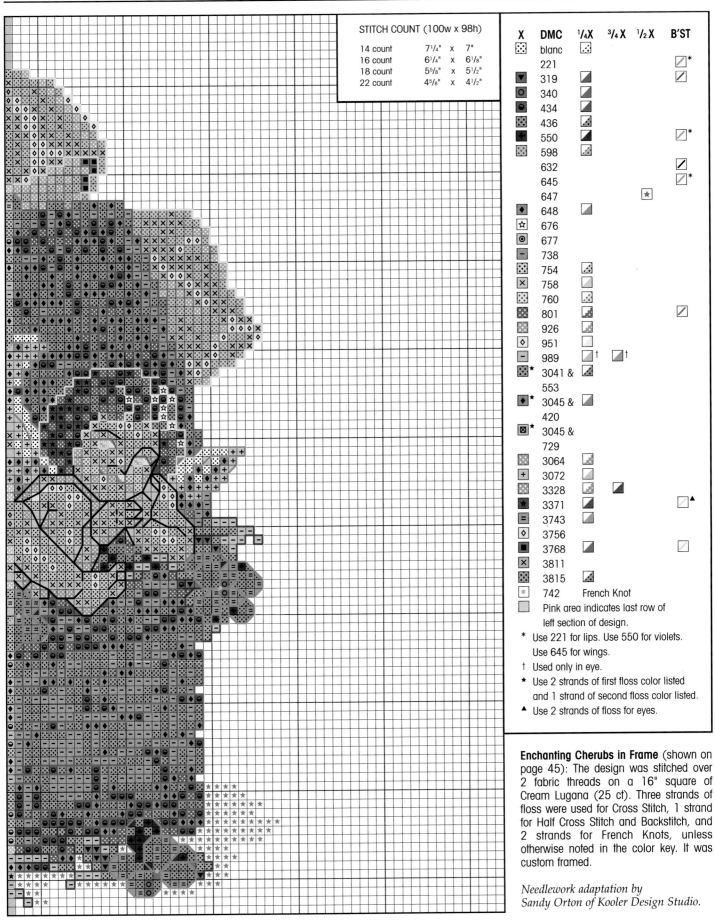

STITCH COUNT (100w x 98h)		
14 count	7¼"	x 7"
16 count	6¼"	x 6⅛"
18 count	5⅝"	x 5½"
22 count	4⅝"	x 4½"

X	DMC	¼X	¾X	½X	B'ST
⠿	blanc	⠿			
	221				⧄*
▼	319	◣			⧄
◎	340	◣			
◪	434	◪			
⠿	436	◪			
◆	550	◣			⧄*
⠿	598	◪			
	632				⧄
	645				⧄*
	647			★	
◆	648	◣			
☆	676				
◉	677				
−	738				
⠿	754	⠿			
✕	758	◱			
⠿	760	◪			
⠿	801	◪			⧄
⠿	926	◣			
◇	951	▢			
−	989	◣†	◣†		
⠿★	3041 &	◣			
	553				
◆	3045 &	◣			
	420				
⊠★	3045 &	◪			
	729				
⠿	3064	◣			
+	3072	◣			
⠿	3328	◣	◣		
★	3371	◣			⧄▲
=	3743	◣			
◇	3756				
■	3768	◣			⧄
✕	3811				
⠿	3815	◪			
●	742	French Knot			

Pink area indicates last row of
left section of design.

* Use 221 for lips. Use 550 for violets.
Use 645 for wings.

† Used only in eye.

* Use 2 strands of first floss color listed
and 1 strand of second floss color listed.

▲ Use 2 strands of floss for eyes.

Enchanting Cherubs in Frame (shown on page 45): The design was stitched over 2 fabric threads on a 16" square of Cream Lugana (25 ct). Three strands of floss were used for Cross Stitch, 1 strand for Half Cross Stitch and Backstitch, and 2 strands for French Knots, unless otherwise noted in the color key. It was custom framed.

Needlework adaptation by
Sandy Orton of Kooler Design Studio.

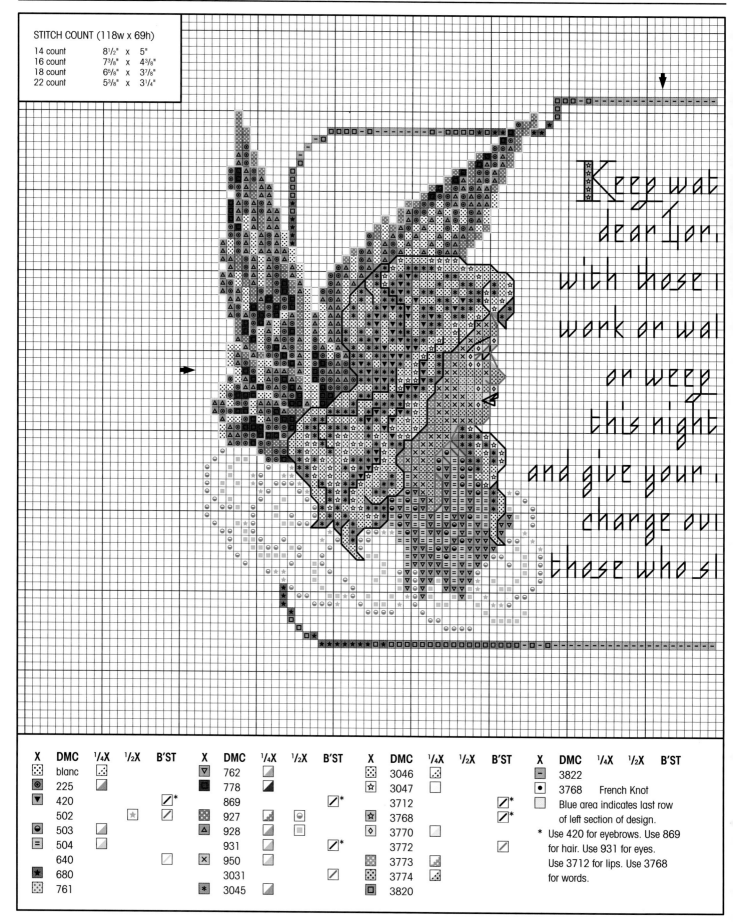

STITCH COUNT (118w x 69h)

14 count	8½"	x	5"
16 count	7⅜"	x	4⅜"
18 count	6⅝"	x	3⅞"
22 count	5⅜"	x	3¼"

Keep wat dear Lor, with those I work or wal or weep this night and give your, charge ou those who sl

X	DMC	¼X	½X	B'ST	X	DMC	¼X	½X	B'ST	X	DMC	¼X	½X	B'ST	X	DMC	¼X	½X	B'ST
	blanc					762					3046					3822			
	225					778					3047					3768			French Knot
	420			✓*		869			✓*		3712			✓*		Blue area indicates last row			
	502					927					3768			✓*		of left section of design.			
	503					928					3770					* Use 420 for eyebrows. Use 869			
	504					931			✓*		3772			✓		for hair. Use 931 for eyes.			
	640					950					3773					Use 3712 for lips. Use 3768			
	680					3031					3774					for words.			
	761					3045					3820								

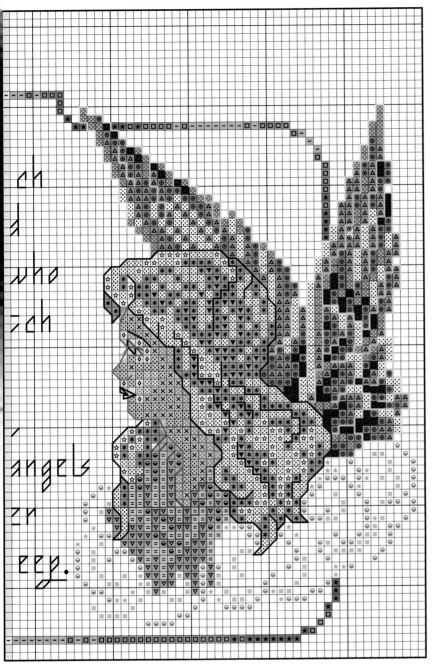

Watchful Angels in Frame (shown on page 47): The design was stitched over two fabric threads on a 15" x 12" piece of Antique White Lugana (25 ct). Three strands of floss were used for Cross Stitch and 1 strand for Half Cross Stitch, Backstitch, and French Knot. It was custom framed.

Watchful Angel Hanging Pillow (shown on page 49): The angel and cloud from right side of the design were stitched on a 12" x 13" piece of Antique White Aida (16 ct). Two strands of floss were used for Cross Stitch and 1 strand for Half Cross Stitch and Backstitch.

For pillow, you will need a 5¹/₂" x 6¹/₂" piece of fabric for pillow backing, 5¹/₂" x 41" fabric strip for ruffle, 2" x 22" bias fabric strip for cording, 22" length of ¹/₄" dia. purchased cord, two 12" lengths of ¹/₂"w ribbon for bows, two 18" lengths of ¹/₂"w ribbon for hanger, and polyester fiberfill.

Centering design, trim stitched piece to measure 5¹/₂" x 6¹/₂".

Center cord on wrong side of bias strip; matching long edges, fold strip over cord. Use a zipper foot to baste along length of strip close to cord; trim seam allowance to ¹/₂". Matching raw edges, pin cording to right side of stitched piece, making a ³/₈" clip in seam allowance of cording at corners. Ends of cording should overlap approximately 2"; pin overlapping end out of the way. Starting 2" from beginning end of cording and ending 4" from overlapping end, baste cording to stitched piece. On overlapping end of cording, remove 2¹/₂" of basting; fold end of fabric back and trim cord so that it meets beginning end of cord. Fold end of fabric ¹/₂" to wrong side; wrap fabric over beginning end of cording. Finish basting cording to stitched piece.

For ruffle, press short edges of fabric strip ¹/₂" to wrong side. Matching wrong sides and long edges, fold strip in half; press. Machine baste ¹/₂" from raw edges; gather fabric strip to fit stitched piece. Matching raw edges, pin ruffle to right side of stitched piece, overlapping short ends ¹/₄". Use a ¹/₂" seam allowance to sew ruffle to stitched piece.

Matching right sides and leaving an opening for turning, use a ¹/₂" seam allowance to sew stitched piece and backing fabric together. Trim seam allowances diagonally at corners; turn pillow right side out, carefully pushing corners outward. Stuff pillow with polyester fiberfill and blind stitch opening closed. Tie each 12" length of ribbon in a bow. Referring to photo, tack one 18" length of ribbon and one bow to each upper corner of pillow; trim ends and tie hanger in a bow.

Needlework adaptation by Donna Vermillion Giampa.

FINISHING INSTRUCTIONS

Tulip Candle Tie Finishing (shown on page 22; chart on page 69): For candle tie, you will need a 9" square of lightweight white fabric for backing, fabric stiffener, small foam brush, 34" length of 1¹/₂"w sheer ribbon, 34" length of 2¹/₂"w sheer wired ribbon, 16" length of ¹/₁₆"w ribbon, 4" x 6" candle, and clear-drying craft glue.

To stiffen design, follow Stiffening Instructions, page 83; cut out close to edges of stitched design. Holding both 34" lengths of ribbon together and referring to photo, tie a bow around candle. Tie 16" length of ribbon in a bow; referring to photo, glue stiffened design and bow to center of bow on candle. Trim all ribbon ends as desired.

Daffodil Plant Poke Finishing (shown on page 22; chart on page 69): For plant poke, you will need a 9" square of lightweight white fabric for backing, fabric stiffener, small foam brush, two 14" lengths of 1¹/₂"w sheer ribbon, 10" length of ¹/₈" dia. bamboo skewer, and clear drying craft glue.

To stiffen design, follow Stiffening Instructions, page 83; cut out close to edges of stitched design. Holding both lengths of ribbon together, tie in a bow; trim ends as desired. Referring to photo, glue stiffened design and bow to skewer.

Violet Bookmark Finishing (shown on page 22; chart on page 69): For bookmark, you will need a 9" square of lightweight white fabric for backing, fabric stiffener, small foam brush, 25" length of 1¹/₂"w sheer ribbon, one 14" length each of ¹/₄"w, ¹/₈"w, and ¹/₁₆"w ribbon, and clear-drying craft glue.

To stiffen design, follow Stiffening Instructions, page 83; cut out close to edges of stitched design. Matching short ends, fold 25" length of ribbon in half. Holding all 14" lengths of ribbon together, tie in a bow around sheer ribbon 1¹/₂" from folded edge; trim all ribbon ends as desired. Referring to photo, glue stiffened design to sheer ribbon.

home sweet haven

#1 (57w x 27h)

#2 (79w x 57h)

For a good angel
will go with him
This journey will
be successful
and he will
come home
safe and sound
TOBIAS 5:21

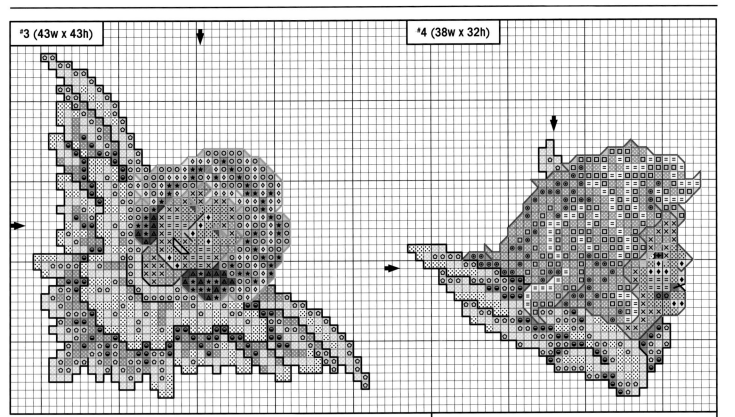

#3 (43w x 43h) **#4 (38w x 32h)**

Angelic Trio Towel (shown on page 49): Design #1 was stitched on the Aida (14 ct) border of a White Velour Fingertip™ towel. Three strands of floss were used for Cross Stitch and 1 strand for Backstitch.

Journey Angel in Frame (shown on page 48): Design #2 was stitched on a 12" x 10" piece of Antique White Aida (14 ct). Three strands of floss were used for Cross Stitch and 1 strand for Backstitch. It was custom framed.

Angel Bread Cloth (shown on page 48): Design #3 was stitched on one corner of a White Bread Cover (14 ct) with design 7 squares from beginning of fringe. Three strands of floss were used for Cross Stitch and 1 strand for Backstitch.

Angelic Porcelain Jar (shown on page 49): Design #4 was stitched on an 8" square of Antique White Aida (14 ct). Three strands of floss were used for Cross Stitch and 1 strand for Backstitch. It was inserted in the lid of a 5" dia. porcelain jar (3½" dia. opening).

Needlework adaptations by Donna Vermillion Giampa.

X	DMC	¼X	B'ST		X	DMC	¼X	B'ST
	blanc				=	3047		
	300		/*			3328		/*
*	301	/				3708		
◉	420	/				3712		
▲	433	/			□	3721		/†
	434		/			3743	/	
★	435	/			✧	3756		
◉	437	/				3761		
	640		/†			3766	/	
◇	738				◆	3770		
	747					3772		/
=	761					3773	/	
×	762	/				3774		
◉	807	/				3776	/	
▼	839	/	/†		☆	3782	/	
▲	840	/				3809		/*
	869		/		◆	3811	/	
◆	930		/*					
	931	/						
×	950	/						
◆	975	/						
	3031		/					
	3041		/*					
◉	3042	/						
	3045	/						
□	3046	/						

* Use 300 for hair. Use 930 for eye. Use 3328 for mouth. Use 3041 for gown. Use 3809 for words on Design #2 and for wings on Designs #3 and #4.

† Use 640 for wings. Use 839 for eyes. Use 3721 for mouths.

FINISHING INSTRUCTIONS

Violet Shower Pillow Finishing (shown on page 23; chart on page 68): For pillow, you will need an 8¼" square of fabric for pillow backing, 6" x 65" fabric strip for ruffle (pieced as necessary), 2" x 34" bias fabric strip for cording, 34" length of ¼" dia. purchased cord, and polyester fiberfil.

Centering design, trim stitched piece to measure 8¼" square.

Center cord on wrong side of bias strip; matching long edges, fold strip over cord. Use a zipper foot to baste along length of strip close to cord; trim seam allowance to ½". Matching raw edges, pin cording to right side of stitched piece, making a ⅜"clip in seam allowance of cording at corners. Ends of cording should overlap approximately 2"; pin overlapping end out of the way. Starting 2" from beginning end of cording and ending 4" from overlapping end, baste cording to stitched piece. On overlapping end of cording, remove 2½" of basting; fold end of fabric back and trim cord so that it meets beginning end of cord. Fold end of fabric ½" to wrong side; wrap fabric over beginning end of cording. Finish basting cording to stitched piece.

For ruffle, press short edges of fabric strip ½" to wrong side. Matching wrong sides and long edges, fold strip in half; press. Machine baste ½" from raw edges; gather fabric strip to fit stitched piece. Matching raw edges, pin ruffle to right side of stitched piece, overlapping short ends ¼". Use a ½" seam allowance to sew ruffle to stitched piece.

Matching right sides and leaving an opening for turning, use a ½" seam allowance to sew stitched piece and backing fabric together. Trim seam allowances diagonally at corners; turn pillow right side out, carefully pushing corners outward. Stuff pillow with polyester fiberfill and blind stitch opening closed.

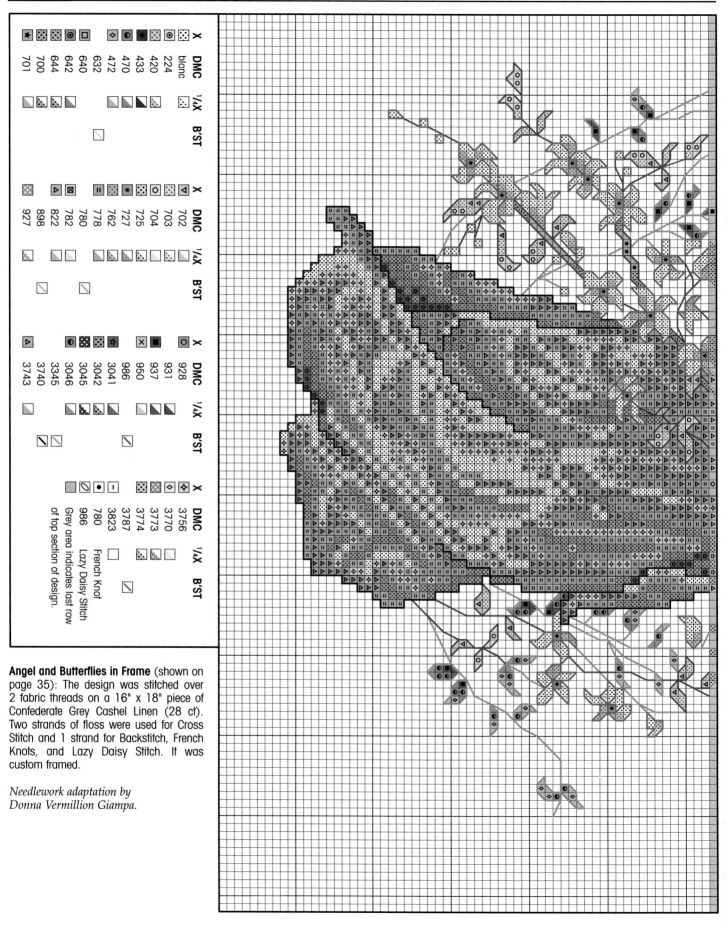

Angel and Butterflies in Frame (shown on page 35): The design was stitched over 2 fabric threads on a 16" x 18" piece of Confederate Grey Cashel Linen (28 ct). Two strands of floss were used for Cross Stitch and 1 strand for Backstitch, French Knots, and Lazy Daisy Stitch. It was custom framed.

Needlework adaptation by Donna Vermillion Giampa.

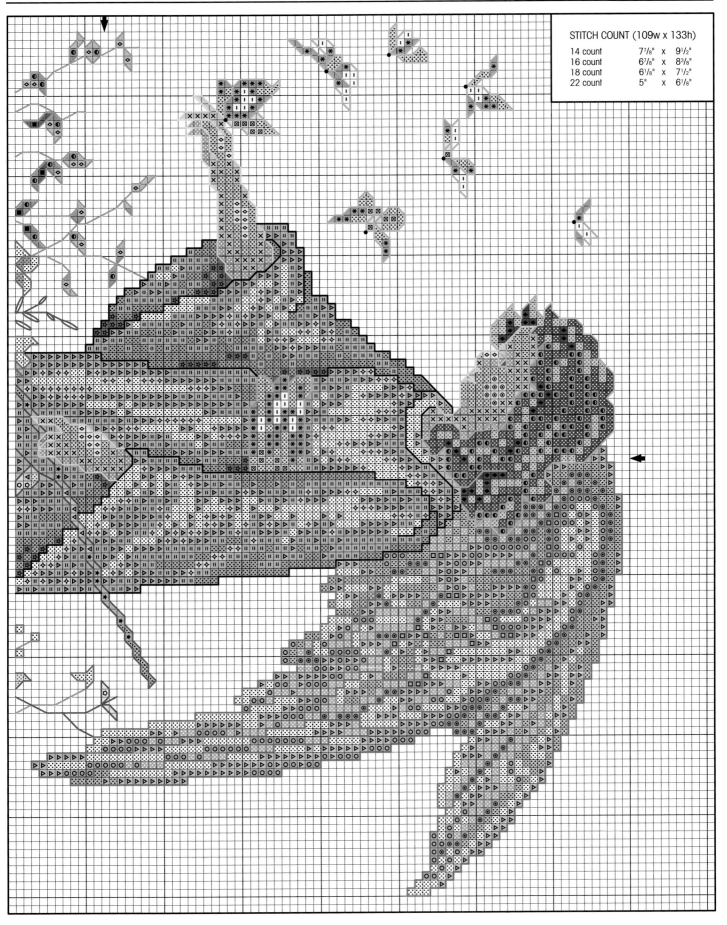

STITCH COUNT (109w x 133h)

14 count	7⁷⁄₈"	x	9¹⁄₂"
16 count	6⁷⁄₈"	x	8³⁄₈"
18 count	6¹⁄₈"	x	7¹⁄₂"
22 count	5"	x	6¹⁄₈"

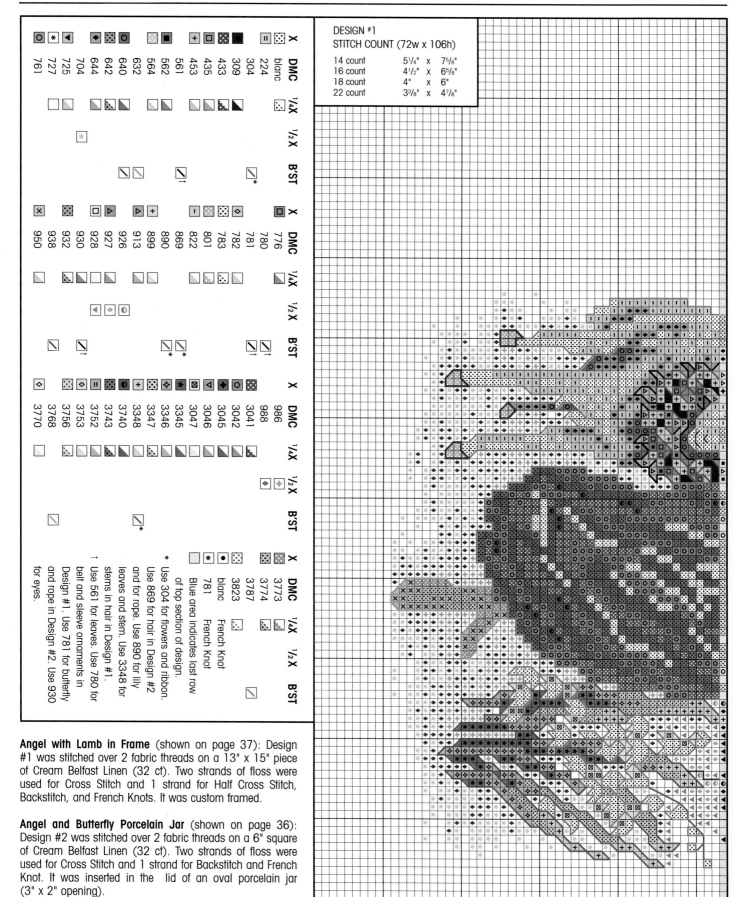

DESIGN #1
STITCH COUNT (72w x 106h)

14 count	5¼"	x 7⅝"
16 count	4½"	x 6⅝"
18 count	4"	x 6"
22 count	3⅜"	x 4⅞"

Color key (X, ¼X, ½X, B'ST, DMC):

DMC: 761, 727, 725, 704, 644, 642, 640, 632, 564, 562, 561, 453, 435, 433, 309, 304, 224, blanc

DMC: 950, 938, 932, 930, 928, 927, 926, 913, 899, 890, 869, 822, 801, 783, 782, 781, 780, 776

DMC: 3770, 3768, 3756, 3753, 3752, 3743, 3740, 3348, 3347, 3346, 3345, 3047, 3046, 3045, 3042, 3041, 988, 986

DMC: 3773, 3774, 3787, 3823

blanc — French Knot
781 — French Knot

* Blue area indicates last row of top section of design.
Use 304 for flowers and ribbon. Use 869 for hair in Design #2 and for rope. Use 890 for lily leaves and stem. Use 3348 for stems in hair in Design #1.

† Use 561 for leaves. Use 780 for belt and sleeve ornaments in Design #1. Use 781 for butterfly and rope in Design #2. Use 930 for eyes.

Angel with Lamb in Frame (shown on page 37): Design #1 was stitched over 2 fabric threads on a 13" x 15" piece of Cream Belfast Linen (32 ct). Two strands of floss were used for Cross Stitch and 1 strand for Half Cross Stitch, Backstitch, and French Knots. It was custom framed.

Angel and Butterfly Porcelain Jar (shown on page 36): Design #2 was stitched over 2 fabric threads on a 6" square of Cream Belfast Linen (32 ct). Two strands of floss were used for Cross Stitch and 1 strand for Backstitch and French Knot. It was inserted in the lid of an oval porcelain jar (3" x 2" opening).

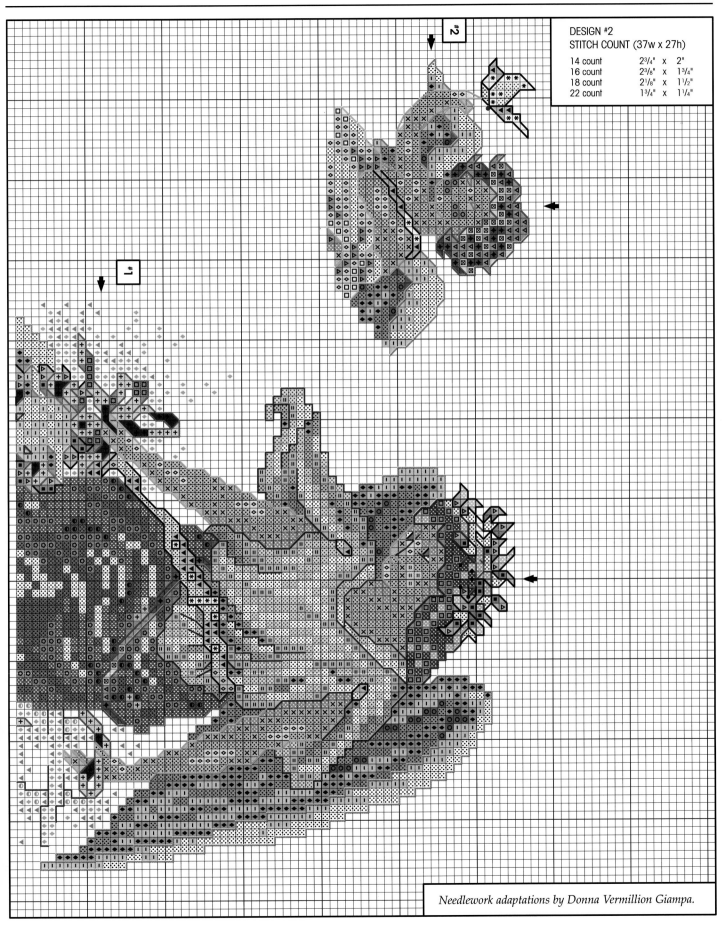

DESIGN #2
STITCH COUNT (37w x 27h)

14 count	2³/₄" x	2"
16 count	2³/₈" x	1³/₄"
18 count	2¹/₈" x	1¹/₂"
22 count	1³/₄" x	1¹/₄"

#2

#1

Needlework adaptations by Donna Vermillion Giampa.

Angel with Dove in Frame
(shown on page 36): The design was stitched over 2 fabric threads on a 16" x 14" piece of Confederate Grey Cashel Linen (28 ct). Three strands of floss were used for Cross Stitch and 1 strand for Backstitch and French Knots. It was custom framed.

Needlework adaptation by Donna Vermillion Giampa.

STITCH COUNT (108w x 81h)

14 count	7³/₄"	x	5⁷/₈"
16 count	6³/₄"	x	5¹/₈"
18 count	6"	x	4¹/₂"
22 count	5"	x	3³/₄"

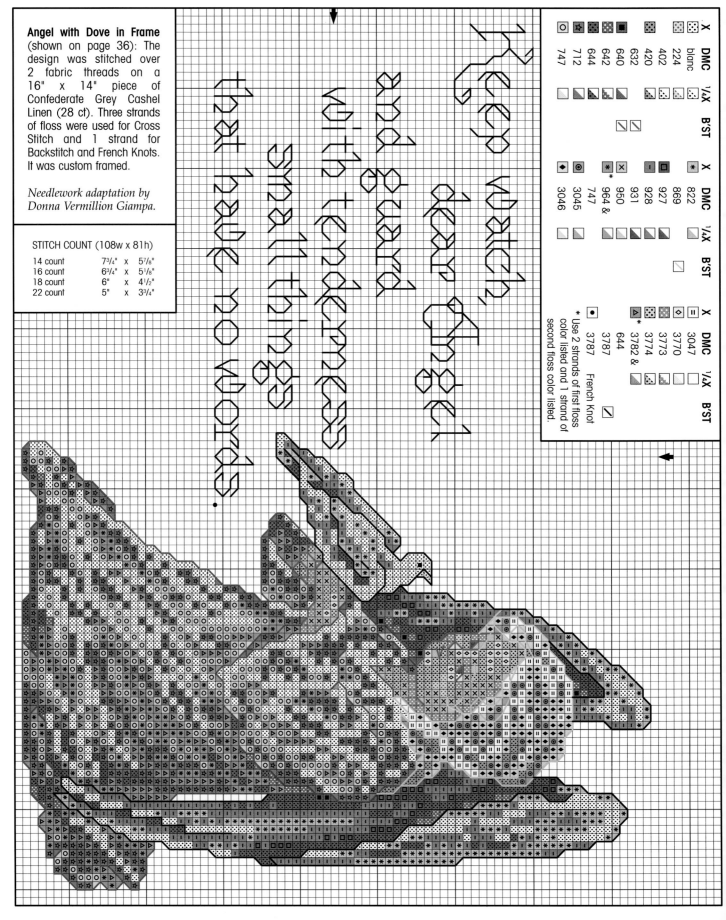

GENERAL INSTRUCTIONS

WORKING WITH CHARTS

How to Read Charts: Each of the designs is shown in chart form. Each colored square on the chart represents one Cross Stitch or one Half Cross Stitch. Each colored triangle on the chart represents one One-Quarter Stitch or one Three-Quarter Stitch. Black or colored dots represent French Knots or bead placement. Colored ovals represent Lazy Daisy Stitches. The black or colored straight lines on the chart indicate Backstitch. When a French Knot, Lazy Daisy Stitch, or Backstitch covers a square, the symbol is omitted.

Each chart is accompanied by a color key. This key indicates the color of floss to use for each stitch on the chart. The headings on the color key are for Cross Stitch (**X**), DMC color number (**DMC**), One-Quarter Stitch (**¼X**), Three-Quarter Stitch (**¾X**), Half Cross Stitch (**½X**), and Backstitch (**B'ST**). Color key columns should be read vertically and horizontally to determine type of stitch and floss color. Some designs may include stitches worked with metallic thread, such as Blending Filament, blended with floss. If any metallic thread is used in a design, the color key will contain the necessary information.

Where to Start: The horizontal and vertical centers of each charted design are shown by arrows. You may start at any point on the charted design, but be sure the design will be centered on the fabric. Locate the center of fabric by folding in half, top to bottom and again left to right. On the charted design, count the number of squares (stitches) from the center of the chart to where you wish to start. Then, from the fabric's center, find your starting point by counting out the same number of fabric threads (stitches). (**Note:** To work over two fabric threads, count out twice the number of fabric threads.)

How to Determine Finished Size: The finished size of your design will depend on the **thread count per inch** of the fabric being used. To determine the finished size of the design on different fabrics, divide the number of squares (stitches) in the width of the charted design by the thread count of the fabric. For example, a charted design with a width of 80 squares worked on 14 count Aida will yield a design 5¾" wide. Repeat for the number of squares (stitches) in the height of the charted design. (**Note:** To work over two fabric threads, divide the number of squares by one-half the thread count.) Then add the amount of background you want plus a generous amount for finishing. Whipstitch or zigzag the edges of your fabric to prevent raveling.

STITCH DIAGRAMS

Note: Bring threaded needle up at 1 and all odd numbers and down at 2 and all even numbers.

Counted Cross Stitch (X): Work one Cross Stitch to correspond to each colored square on the chart. For horizontal rows, work stitches in two journeys (**Fig. 1**). For vertical rows, complete each stitch as shown (**Fig. 2**). When working over two fabric threads, work Cross Stitch as shown in **Fig. 3**. When the chart shows a Backstitch crossing a colored square (**Fig. 4**), a Cross Stitch should be worked first; then the Backstitch (**Fig. 9 or 10**) should be worked on top of the Cross Stitch.

Fig. 1

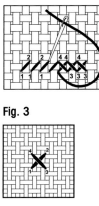

Fig. 2

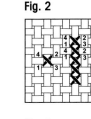

Fig. 3

Fig. 4

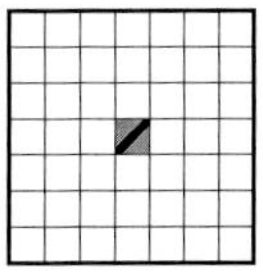

Quarter Stitch (¼X and ¾X): Quarter Stitches are denoted by triangular shapes of color on the chart and on the color key. For a One-Quarter Stitch, come up at 1 (**Fig. 5**); split fabric thread to go down at 2. When stitches 1-4 are worked in the same color, the resulting stitch is called a Three-Quarter Stitch (**¾X**). **Fig. 6** shows the technique for Quarter Stitches when working over two fabric threads.

Fig. 5

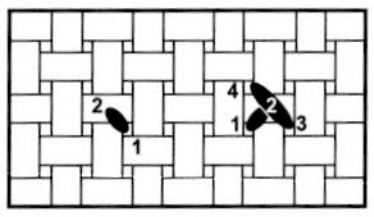

Fig. 6

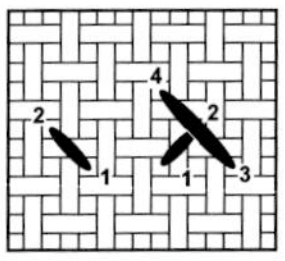

Half Cross Stitch (½X): This stitch is one journey of the Cross Stitch and is worked from lower left to upper right as shown in **Fig. 7**. When working over two fabric threads, work Half Cross Stitch as shown in **Fig. 8**.

Fig. 7

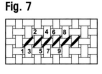

Fig. 8

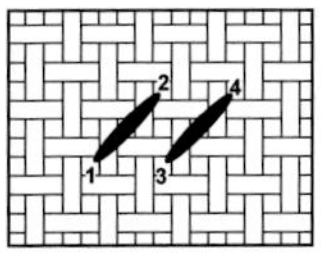

Backstitch (B'ST): For outline detail, Backstitch (shown on chart and on color key by black or colored straight lines) should be worked after the design has been completed (**Fig. 9**). When working over two fabric threads, work Backstitch as shown in **Fig. 10**.

Fig. 9

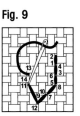

Fig. 10

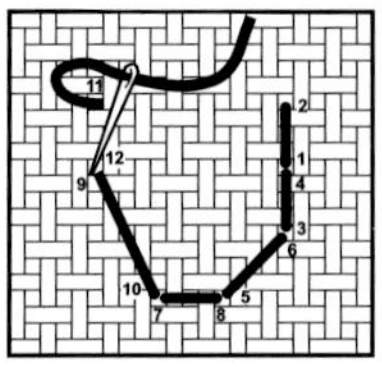

French Knot: Bring needle up at 1. Wrap floss once around needle and insert needle at 2, holding end of floss with non-stitching fingers (**Fig. 11**). Tighten knot; pull needle through fabric, holding floss until it must be released. For larger knot, use more strands of floss; wrap only once.

Fig. 11

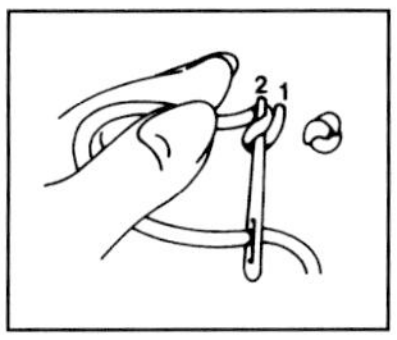

Lazy Daisy Stitch: Bring needle up at 1 and make a loop. Go down at 1 and come up at 2, keeping floss below point of needle (**Fig. 12**). Pull needle through and go down at 2 to anchor loop, completing stitch. (**Note:** To support stitches, it may be helpful to go down in edge of next fabric thread when anchoring loop.)

Fig. 12

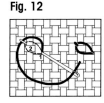

Continued on page 96.

95

STITCHING TIPS

Working over Two Fabric Threads: Use the sewing method instead of the stab method when working over two fabric threads. To use the sewing method, keep your stitching hand on the right side of the fabric (instead of stabbing the fabric with the needle and taking your stitching hand to the back of the fabric to pick up the needle). With the sewing method, take the needle down and up with one stroke instead of two. To add support to stitches, it is important that the first Cross Stitch is placed on the fabric with stitch 1-2 beginning and ending at a point where a vertical fabric thread crosses over a horizontal fabric thread (**Fig. 13**). When the first stitch is in the correct position, the entire design will be placed properly, with vertical fabric threads supporting each stitch.

Fig. 13

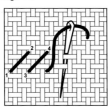

Attaching Beads: Refer to chart for bead placement and sew bead in place using a fine needle that will pass through bead. Bring needle up at 1, run needle through bead and then down at 2. Secure floss on back or move to next bead as shown in **Fig. 14**.

Fig. 14

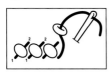

SILK RIBBON EMBROIDERY

The following information will enable you to recreate the effect achieved in the bouquet of **Bride's Blessing in Frame** (shown on page 25; chart on pages 70-71) by working embroidery stitches using silk ribbon. The cross stitches for the roses were omitted; the leaves and streamers were worked on top of the cross stitches.

GENERAL INFORMATION

Ribbon: Ribbons, either 100% silk or synthetic, are available in many colors, widths, and brands. The most commonly used widths are 2mm, 4mm, and 7mm.

Needle: For ribbon, use a sharp-pointed needle with a long eye which allows ribbon to slip through easily. A size 18 chenille needle is recommended. For French Knots, use a sharp needle with a smaller eye than the chenille needle. A size 7 crewel needle is recommended.

Threading Needle with Ribbon: Cut a 14" length of ribbon; thread ribbon through eye of needle. Bring ribbon end to point of needle, piercing ribbon approximately 1/4" from end (**Fig. 15a**). Pull short end of ribbon down over eye of needle; gently pull long end, securing ribbon to needle (**Fig. 15b**).

Fig. 15a   **Fig. 15b**

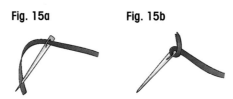

Beginning and Ending with Ribbon: To begin, form a soft knot in ribbon by folding ribbon end back approximately 1/4" and piercing ribbon through both layers (**Fig. 16a**). Gently pull ribbon through to form a knot (**Fig 16b**). To end, secure end of ribbon on wrong side of fabric by making a knot.

Fig. 16a   **Fig. 16b**

STITCHING INSTRUCTIONS

Referring to Pattern for placement of stitches and following stitch diagrams, work silk ribbon embroidery bouquet in the following order.

Couched Ribbon Streamers:
This stitch is represented on Pattern as [● ● ●].

Cut a 14" length of cream 4mm ribbon. Come up at one end of streamer, twist ribbon as desired and anchor with French Knots (**Fig. 11**) using DMC ecru floss. Take ribbon to back of stitched piece at opposite end of streamer (**Fig. 17**).

Fig. 17

Japanese Ribbon Stitch Leaves:
This stitch is represented on Pattern as 🍂.

Cut a 14" length of green 4mm ribbon. Come up at 1. Lay ribbon flat on fabric and go down at 2, piercing ribbon (**Fig. 18a**). Gently pull needle to back of stitched piece. Do not pull ribbon tightly; ribbon will curl at tip as shown in **Fig. 18b**.

Fig. 18a   **Fig. 18b**

Spider Web Roses:
This stitch is represented on Pattern as

Using one strand of DMC ecru floss, come up a odd numbers and go down at even numbers t work five straight stitches to form ancho stitches (**Fig 19a**). Cut a 14" length of light pin 4mm ribbon. Coming up at center, use ribbo to weave over and under anchor stitche (**Fig 19b**), allowing ribbon to twist and keepin ribbon loose. Continue to weave until ancho stitches are covered halfway out from cente point. Take ribbon to back of stitched piec under an anchor thread. Cut a 14" length c cream 4mm ribbon; come up where previou ribbon color was taken to back of stitched piec Continue weaving ribbon in same manner unt anchor stitches are covered.

Fig. 19a   **Fig. 19b**

PATTERN

Grey area on Pattern represents roses omitte from stitched piece (chart on pages 70-71).

Instructions tested and photo items made by Kan Ashford, Marsha Besancon, Vicky Bishop, Alic Crowder, Vanessa Edwards, Jody Fuller, Elair Garrett, Joyce Graves, Nelwyn Gray, Judy Grim, Chr Harvey, Muriel Hicks, Joyce Holland, Elizabe James, Arthur Jungnickel, Melanie Long, Phyll Lundy, Karen Matthew, Susan McDonald, Ray Elle Odle, Patricia O'Neil, Angie Perryman, Cynth Sanders, Susan Sego, Lavonne Sims, Helen Stanto and Trish Vines.